Book One in the
On a Wing and a Prayer series

Just a Little Higher

A collection of true stories about women and the special birds who encouraged them

Linda Franklin

TEACH Services, Inc.
PUBLISHING
www.TEACHServices.com • (800) 367-1844

World rights reserved. This book or any portion thereof may not be copied or reproduced in any form or manner whatsoever, except as provided by law, without the written permission of the publisher, except by a reviewer who may quote brief passages in a review.

The author assumes full responsibility for the accuracy of all facts and quotations as cited in this book. The opinions expressed in this book are the author's personal views and interpretations, and do not necessarily reflect those of the publisher.

This book is provided with the understanding that the publisher is not engaged in giving spiritual, legal, medical, or other professional advice. If authoritative advice is needed, the reader should seek the counsel of a competent professional.

Copyright © 2018 Linda Franklin
Copyright © 2018 TEACH Services, Inc.
ISBN-13: 978-1-4796-0936-9 (Paperback)
ISBN-13: 978-1-4796-0937-6 (ePub)
Library of Congress Control Number: 2018963002

Comfort comes on soft little wings just when these women need it most!

Edited by Linda Marie Harrington Steinke.

Scriptures are taken from the King James Version of the Bible. Public domain.

Illustrated by Duncan Long.

Published by

www.TEACHServices.com • (800) 367-1844

Other books by Linda Franklin

On a Wing and a Prayer series

Book Two: *Staying Aloft*—True stories about men and the extraordinary birds who loved them.

Book Three: *Climbing the Heights*—Never before published true and inspirational bird stories.

Book Four: *Such Sweet Songs*—Listen carefully! The song of a bird can heal a wounded heart!

Rainbow series

Book One: *Rainbow in the Flames*—A tragic fire, a bow of promise, a love of the lasting kind. The healing journey of an optimistic burn survivor (color photos).

Book Two: *Shadows Point to Rainbows*—The remarkable journey of a devoted dog and his beloved boy.

Book Three: *Johnny Sundown*—A wild trapper discovers solace in Canada's Peace Country.

Survival series

Book One: *Country in My Heart*—Success stories of people who prayed for a country home. Compiled and edited by Jere and Linda Franklin (b/w photos).

Dedication

This book is dedicated to my mother,

Lilly Loretta Harper

who taught me to love good stories, laughter, beauty, and God.

Contents

To the Reader . . . . *vii*

Introduction . . . . *ix*

Stories

Seven Little Feathers 13

Rainbow in the Dark 22

Charlie's Home 31

Kiwi 43

Once Upon a Song 51

Pigeon Toes 57

The Open Cage 65

Trill 74

The Sparrow's Song 81

Out of My Shell 87

A Rooster Named Benedict—*Penny Porter* 93

Poems and Quotes

Faith—*Victor Hugo* 21

A Farewell—*Charles Kingsley*. 29

Charlie's Home—Forevermore!—*Linda Franklin* 41

Overheard in an Orchard—*Elizabeth Cheney* 50

The Gulls—*Linda Franklin* .56

Our Heroes—Phoebe Cary. 64

Under His Wings—*W. O. Cushing* 73

Into the Light—*E. White* 80

His Eye Is on the Sparrow—*Civilla D. Martin*. 83

A Perfect World—*L. Franklin* 86

Silent Sounds—*Jon Kiefiuk*. 91

Farther Along—*W. B. Stevens/W. A. Fletcher* 100

To the Reader

Difficult times call for serious joy. This compilation is filled with true accounts about women who, helpless to overcome impossible situations, were helped by birds. The timing of the visit seemed to be ordained; their little angel came exactly when their encouragement was most needed. Not only was the winged messenger sent with good news, it was bundled in such irresistible beauty of form and character that there remained no doubt as to *who* had sent it! I feel privileged to have been chosen to chronicle these uplifting stories.

Next time a trial comes your way, watch and be ready! There may be a pair of soft little wings waiting to lift *your* spirit *just a little higher.*

Introduction

My mother loves beauty. My earliest memories are of the two of us picking bouquets of tiger lilies and trilliums together and listening to the robins singing in the tall Douglas fir trees that surrounded our house in the suburbs of Portland, Oregon.

As her little flock expanded, Mamma gathered the four of us around her for story time, urging us to memorize quotations from the Bible and classic literature. It was during one of these nightly readings that I first heard and memorized my favorite poem about beauty.

> If, of thy mortal goods, thou art bereft,
> And from thy slender store
> Two loaves alone to thee are left,
> Sell one and from the dole,
> Buy hyacinths to feed thy soul.
>
> —*Sadi*

Though she treasured the written word, singing was one of Mamma's favorite expressions. Most often she sang hymns, but when a difficult situation was miraculously resolved, I would sometimes hear her murmur a few words from a World War II song, "On a Wing and a Prayer." It was a mysterious saying. I never understood, until much later, that its origin had to do with the survival of an injured "war bird"—find the story the introductory remarks in book two of this series—and it may well have launched my profound respect of birds at an early age. *Can the beautiful wings of a bird actually hold a prayer?* I could never resist inspecting the feathers I found; beauty, birds, and prayer were allies. However rough life's trail might be, finding a feather always launched my thoughts *just a little higher*.

The deprivations of the Great Depression launched Mamma's quest for refinement. The rough boards on her childhood home, a scantily furnished house in eastern Oregon, failed to block the severe winter winds, but Mamma was more than just a survivor. She carved out a delicate niche among her eleven siblings, maintaining her dignity by refashioning her hand-me-down clothing and teaching herself shorthand to augment the basic typing skills offered at Lostine High School. It was not just her manual skills that made Mamma a valuable executive secretary. She seemed to automatically visualize the potential for beauty in every person she met and every room she remodeled.

I grew up thinking that all mothers could look at a picture in a magazine and transform a delapidated house into a beautiful home, in a short time, with a minimal outlay of cash. Before I hit first grade, Mamma had taught me to sand and paint *with* the grain of the wood, never *against* it. When we moved to the city to restore a large house that had fallen into disrepair, I wondered why the other mothers in our neighborhood did not at least wash their windows and scrape the flaking paint from their houses. Was it not it a woman's God-given role to beautify the world by painting, wallpapering, refinishing, updating, and landscaping?

Mamma taught her children to set the table properly, carefully placing the spoon and knife on the right, the fork on the left. Meals at home, whether sack lunches or Thanksgiving dinners, were neat and artistic. We never tasted dessert until the table was cleared and set again *properly*, but Mamma always made it clear that a thankful heart was more important than pretty place settings or fine food. "Things do not dictate worth," she would tell us "but we must take care of what we have." She made

Introduction

it clear that our value system was to include character growth. We were never allowed to indulge in prejudicial commentary based on appearance, nationality, religion, illness, or physical limitations.

As the oldest of her four nestlings, I should have discerned the challenges Mamma faced when budgetary needs dictated that she work a part-time evening shift and it fell my lot to have supper ready for the family. How could a teenager compete with those amazing cooking skills? What I lacked in finesse, I decided to (over) compensate with color: a serving of mashed potatoes might be brilliant green or resemble my favorite confetti angel-food cake with red, yellow, and blue dots; carrots were a much brighter orange than they came from the Creator's hand; broccoli was a radiant aqua. A vivid dessert, such as graham crackers piled high with flamboyant pink frosting, completed the spectrum. When Daddy cautiously complained, Mamma encouraged me to brighten people's lives in more tasteful methods.

"Color is good, Linda," she gently explained, "but one must not overdo it. As you prepare food, keep in mind its natural beauty. Think of this as you dress, too. Start with simple, clean, and neat, then maybe add one frill."

Within a few weeks of that episode, she designed an artist's smock for me, complete with an appliqué of a felt palette onto which she sewed colorful buttons resembling circles of paint. Then she kept me well supplied with crayons, chalk, watercolors, coloring books, and writing paper. By her consistent example, I learned that true beauty is a resting place for the soul, that capturing it is essential, and that it is easily destroyed by disorder or thoughtlessness. She was never too busy with her own projects not to include someone who was suffering from illness or in need of a spiritual uplift. And Mamma laughed. Rather than stew about accusations or misunderstandings, she most often expressed amusement about relational challenges. By learning to laugh with Mamma, I discovered that joy, like the love of beauty, is a choice.

"You must keep your clothes, your hair, and your feelings under control, Linda," she'd remind me when I too often came home from school in a sour mood, my thick hair flying free of the braids she so carefully crafted each morning, "or they will control you." Outward beauty was not as important to her as was the character I was building. However fine the draperies on my bedroom window, she was careful to remind me that they merely framed the real world in which I would be functioning as a contributing member, not a decoration.

Mamma claimed that television squelched imagination, that drama was not reality, and that children should be outside whenever possible. Her fierce hold on principles of truth made it easy for me to escape peer pressure. I understood that it was okay for me to be different. After the "color lecture," I never again felt the need of artificialities or adjusting my philosophy of life in order to be relevant. I never consciously hungered for acceptance.

When I married and moved to Canada's far north, the beauty of the northern lights that glittered across our vast expanse of snow offered some relief from the whiteness of the long winters, but my love of color lured me into raising canaries. These wonderful birds became the catalyst for recording the personal stories that my customers and friends began sharing with me. Caring for my canaries, I learned a deeper appreciation for their Designer. *Could a feather have been formed by chance?* No, not anymore than you or I could have *happened* by chance! Though the human eye may not immediately discern it, there is a design to all things, even the rocky path on which we all must journey through life.

When I hold a feather in my hand I am reminded that no event is random, that my Designer loves me as I am, but eagerly anticipates the day when I will reflect His image. This is the purpose of the journey. When I cannot see through my tears because of the lesson He seeks to teach, He lovingly redirects my focus—as my mother has so often done—*just a little higher.*

Seven Little Feathers

*Yea the sparrow hath found a house
and the swallow a nest for herself,
where she may lay her young.*

—Psalm 84:3

The setting for this story is the early 1960s in the little town of Irrigon, Oregon, where Lena and Ed Benthin were raising their family. One morning a cheerful little barn swallow tapped on their kitchen door and made known her desire to come inside. Although no one could scientifically explain the reason for the bird's actions, Lena believes that little Sara, understood her need of encouragement. Allowing a bird into her house was as natural to her as adopting a three-legged dog. Everyone and everything felt welcome in that simple country home. Thankfully, my Aunt Lena took time to record Sarah's visit. I am thankful that Lena's sister, my mother, forwarded me Aunt Lena's notes.

One Friday in early June, I saw a few barn swallows flying around the yard at twilight. One bird left the others and fluttered in front of the glass in the door, then it darted back to the window in front of me; it diverted my attention from the dishes I was trying to finish washing in spite of my illness. The bird hung onto the metal rim of the window, flew to the storm door, and then flew back to my window over and over again.

I smiled at these antics as I struggled to finish my chores. I hadn't felt well that day. In fact, I hadn't felt well for several days; I thought I had some kind of flu. The little bird was the only refreshment I'd had all day.

The next day, when I came in from doing the farm chores, I found the same little swallow fighting the storm door ferociously, as if attacking an enemy—this time there was blood on the door. *I must do something to relieve her anxiety!* I thought.

When I opened the storm door, the swallow flew quickly onto the porch, sat on the frame of the door, and began to sing. Soon she was fighting the pane of glass in the back door, obviously wanting to come into the house. I was concerned for her safety, because I could see fresh blood on the window of the inner door.

When I finally opened the door, the swallow did not hesitate—she darted inside. I followed her into the living room and sat down, thankful for the chance to take a little rest. I watched my new guest circle the living room six times, flit through the kitchen and hallway, and hang precariously on the door casings to rest. The flight of this aerial gymnast was graceful and skillful—there was no panic or blood after she came into the house. She stopped just short of the windows, seemingly familiar with the illusions of glass. Sitting calmly on top of a door, she looked down at me and began to sing. The song wrapped around me like a refreshing breeze. I relaxed and felt much better for having stopped to look and listen.

The living room was her favorite place. After singing to me from the top of the door, she preened her wing feathers. Then, graceful as a ballerina, she touched each lovely wing to an outstretched foot.

When she finished stretching, she sang to me again, this time from a curtain rod above the picture window. She was happy to stay with me in the house all day, catching a few flies. About 9:00 p.m., she swooped outside, leaving me to wonder where she would sleep.

On Sunday, she returned, singing joyfully, telling me where she had been and what she had done while we were apart. Though I could not understand what she was saying, I sat and watched her every move and absorbed each sweet note. Her song was good medicine.

Our neighbors came over that evening for supper. When the swallow darted in and flitted through the house, our guests glanced up questioningly. It seemed to me they should be used to these little irregularities in our home, but they looked shocked.

"Oh, that's Sarah," I said, suddenly realizing that our blithe spirit deserved a name. After a prayer for the food, I attempted to break the awkward silence by passing the salad. "First fresh greens of the season," I said.

My neighbor focused on her plate and said, "Isn't that cute?" She wasn't talking about the salad.

"Maybe she's someone's pet," her husband offered, attempting to solve the mystery.

One of the children added a dramatic flair, "She could be sick!"

Throughout the meal, Sarah remained the main topic of conversation. Why had she chosen our house as her own? What was she doing? My neighbors' frowns merely invoked in me a deeper sense of wonder. To me, Sarah was a little angel whose presence seemed to be just what I needed.

On Monday, Sarah appeared to be playing with the drapery rod. Spying something on her beak, I got up from the couch on which I had been resting to take a closer look. I was not expecting what I saw. In spite of my exhaustion, I realized it was time to lay down the law.

"Is that mud on your beak?" I asked, pointing my finger accusingly at her. She looked back at me with perfect innocence. "Oh, no! You are not going to build a nest on that rod. No, you're not!"

Sarah fluttered around my head a couple of times, threw her mud on the floor, and left. *A bird tantrum?* I wondered. She didn't sing to me that day.

On Tuesday, Sarah returned, having obviously forgiven me for my harshness. She was so content—as if living among us was enough to satisfy her every longing.

I was still not feeling well and, as I lay on the couch, Sarah hovered over me as if to ask, "Are you all right?"

It was so very hot that day that I could hardly function. As if sensing that I was not up to mud, Sarah left it outside. Her dainty wings created a cool and welcomed breeze above me. I relaxed; *the rest might do me good*. The last thing I remember before I fell asleep were her two bright eyes looking down on me from the curtain rod. When I awoke, feeling a little better, she chirped cheerfully. She perched quietly on the curtain rod until nightfall and then chirped to me as she darted out the door.

The next day, Wednesday, Sarah flew in and out, talking and singing. No mud! At 9:10 p.m., she sang her goodnight song and then, with a few special chirps directed at me, she flew out into the night.

On Thursday, we went to Heppner. I let Sarah outside and shut the door. When we returned that evening, she was waiting for us and stayed inside until 9:30 p.m., at which time she repeated the song she had sung to me the previous night and left. I was learning swallow talk! Sarah was saying, "Good night! Glad you are feeling a little better! See you tomorrow!"

Uh oh! On Friday, one week after our initial meeting, Sarah flew in with a beak full of mud! I argued with myself, weighing the blood on the door against the mud in her beak. We had a staring contest through the window in the door. I tried to remain firm. Sarah looked directly into my eyes. She won.

When I finally opened the door, she planted a daub of mud on the curtain rod. On return trips, she laid daubs of mud here and there throughout the house, and I began having second thoughts about allowing this little architect into my house. Maybe I was feeling a little better, but I was not up to the mess. I shook my head, sighed, and sat down to rest.

As if reading my mind, Sarah stopped playing with her mud, sat on the top of the door, and began her preening ballet, as if to remind me of how beautiful she was and how privileged I was to have her as a guest. She cleaned herself by swiftly zipping each wing feather through her beak. I was captivated by her gorgeous markings, graceful flight, and colorful attitude.

Again, she chattered happily and sang to me while I rested. At 9:30 p.m., she chirped her now familiar farewell address and swooped out into the darkness.

Sarah flitted in and out of the house all day on Saturday. Her favorite spot was the drapery rod nearest the dining table where the majority of our family activities took place.

She stayed much longer that night. It was dark in the living room, so I turned on the light. She left her perch, swooped through the living room, spied a couple flies on the ceiling, and took care of them for me. Though I was still not strong, I had a chore or two to finish in the kitchen.

Sarah circled my head twice in the kitchen, and went back to her favorite perch. At 9:45 p.m., about the time I finished the supper dishes and began to wonder if she would spend the night, she chirped her farewell greeting and flew away.

Sunday: Bright and early, at 6:30, Sarah hauled in her first serious load of mud. She was in a working mood. Although it didn't look as if she was accomplishing much, she was still working at ten o'clock that evening. I left the door open, turned out the lights, and walked toward my bedroom. In the darkness, I heard her sing her good-night song. I turned and could dimly see her circle the living room twice and then disappear outside.

Monday: Again by 6:30, Sarah was at work hauling mud. She steadily abele mud into her nest until nine o'clock at night, at which time she reexamined her work, sang her goodnight song, then hovered above me chirping an additional message as if to say, "Don't be sad. I'll be back tomorrow, but I might sleep in awhile. It's been a hard day's work!" Then she flew out into the warm summer evening.

Tuesday: Sarah slept in. She didn't start "siding" her nest until 7:00 a.m. Her nest was about an inch and a half high when she began rolling around and around in it, chiseling off pieces of dry mud here a little, there a little, muttering softly to herself as she customized her bed. At 9:00 p.m., her last inspection, she sang us her good-night song, and disappeared into the night.

Wednesday: I heard Sarah before I saw her. She was singing just outside my bedroom window, reminding me that she was ready to begin. At 7:15, when I finally opened the door, she darted into the living room, eager to begin working. Before going to her nest, however, she sat on the drapery rod and sang to me. I appreciated her visit, as I was very weak. I was happy to sit and watch her glide around the room while I rested. She tipped her head from side to side, chirping with a slight inflection as if inquiring about my health.

"Getting better," I answered with a smile. "Thanks to you, Sarah!" She cocked her dainty little head as if seriously considering my answer. Then, tossing me a cheerful chirp, she went to work.

How our family learned to love this little artist! The children sat with me on the couch watching Sarah put the finishing touches on her nest. She had brought in some fine, dry grass with which to line it. She carefully scooped out the rejects, watching them fall onto the carpet below. We all giggled. At 8:45, she sang her good-bye song to us and darted quickly out the door—a little earlier than usual.

Thursday: I went to town early and left the door open for Sarah. She was sitting on the outer doorsill when I returned, as if she was waiting for me. When I came in the house, she flew to her nest and snuggled down in it for the rest of the day, chirping intermittently. At 8:40, she glided silently out into the sultry night.

Friday: Sarah flew to our bedroom window at 6:30, singing and jabbering, but she came in only once that morning, sat in her nest for awhile, and then left. She returned in the afternoon, bringing bits of straw with each trip, then turning around and around in her nest several times to make certain of its comfort. In the evening our two daughters came for a visit. In the process of our visit, I somehow missed Sarah's evening song. Perhaps she didn't bother to sing it to me, seeing that I was busy, or maybe she sensed that my health was improving and that I didn't need the comfort of her song quite as much.

Saturday: Sarah seemed to know, as we packed our car, that the children and I would be leaving for the Carper family reunion in Washington. She did not come into the house when I left the door open for her. My husband, Ed, went to work in Boardman that day. He didn't see Sarah at all, even at suppertime. Although the door remained open, he ate alone. Is Sarah my very own special guest? I went to sleep smiling contentedly at the thought.

Sunday: Sarah was an early bird, apparently happy that I was home again. She sang to me from the window, the door, and then squatted on the rim of her finished nest. She was so cheerful and lovely that I found myself longing for an artist's talent that I might immortalize her indescribable beauty. I know I could not capture her spirit, though, and that is how she claimed my heart. She hovered over the hallway entrance when I emerged from the bedroom, performed a sort of aerial ballet for me, then flew to the kitchen entrance where repeated her fabulous dance for my daughter, Bonnie, then darted outside.

Monday: I felt much better and enjoyed the trip to Heppner with the children. I left the kitchen door open. When we returned at 3:00 p.m., Sarah was gone. At 6:30 in the evening I was still feeling strong enough to walk out to the pasture to check on the cattle. While I was walking through the cows, I saw a noxious weed called dodder. As I was pulling it, a swallow came within a few feet of my head and chattered a steady stream of very anxious swallow talk. I hoped it was Sarah, but I couldn't tell for sure. I returned home, listening intently for her song. The night was quiet, but not peaceful. I missed my little get-well angel.

Tuesday: Dawn was painfully silent. I listened and watched for Sarah. Though my heart was heavy, for the first time in weeks, I felt my energy returning. I was even strong enough to tackle the laundry. One tiny feather on the washing machine reminded me about why I felt empty in spite of my accomplishments. All day I listened, consciously and subconsciously, for my little Sarah. As I hung out the laundry, I found six more feathers on the lawn and put them in the pocket of my apron.

After Sarah was gone for a week, I carefully removed her nest from the curtain rod and placed it in a small birdcage. Wiping my tears, I went around the house cleaning up little spots of mud where she had tested other building sites—three curtain rods, a doorsill, and a battery operated clock—before she had chosen he final location nearest my usual resting place.

I took the feather collection from the shelf in the kitchen where I had been avoiding eye contact with them. Brushing them across the back of my hand, I vividly recalled how Sarah had zipped them efficiently through her beak as she preened and pirouetted on the curtain rod. I placed the feathers inside Sarah's nest and took a quiet moment to consider the memorial. Sarah's fiery spirit, her insistence, her dedication, her beauty, and her sweet songs had meant so much to me. In spite of my sorrow at losing her, I realized that she had given wings to my heart. Would she ever have wanted to become a source of sadness to me? No. What I had given to her? Had I fulfilled her as she had fulfilled me? Oh, how I missed her! Though invisible to other eyes, alongside those seven little feathers was a most precious memory.

Within a few days, the sweetness of the memory outweighed the loss. I was even able to smile when a humorous thought occurred to me. What if Sarah had hatched her babies in our house? What if she had fed them above our table, and taught them to fly in our living room? What if all of Sarah's enthusiastic posterity returned to our house every year instead of the legendary Capistrano migration, as determined as their mother had been to raise their own family? I had to stifle a giggle as I pictured our neighbor's reaction!

One last time, I fondled the seven dainty blue-black feathers and was struck, full force, with the thought that Sarah came to me exactly when I had needed her uplifting influence. With a trust foreign to her nature, this tiny creature of the air shared her joyful spirit, and I would never be the same. Little Sarah had enlarged my heart, just about the width of seven little feathers.

Faith

Be like the bird that,
Pausing in her flight
Awhile on boughs too slight,
Feels them give way
Beneath her and yet sings,
Knowing that she hath wings.

—*Victor Hugo*

Rainbow in the Dark

I call to remembrance my song in the night.

—Psalm 77:6

One day, a longtime friend who was newly widowed asked me to find her a Gouldian finch. Later, when Linda became housebound because of a chemical spill, little Rainbow became her inspiration, perhaps even her salvation. Although she still struggles with a severe breathing disability, her strong faith is an uplifting influence in our small community. I tell her story here as she told it to me—her incredible story of the singing Rainbow.

I now understand why they kill widows in India. After losing Dave, my life became a sort of living death. I knew widowhood would not be easy, but when Dave lost his second battle with cancer, even my training as an LPN had not prepared me for the impact. The smothering shroud of sorrow cast a long, dark shadow over my life. I felt like less than half a person.

Josh, at only eight years of age, lifted more than his share of the burdens and was my inspiration in those early days of our loss. At only eleven months, little Zach was puzzled by his father's absence and my tears. He would toddle over to me and try his best to comfort me. I kept going, mechanically. With no income, I went to work at the local hospital shortly after the funeral and too often found myself in the room where Dave had died. I felt closer to him there—at least closer to the bittersweet memories.

Stepping into room 111, I could always hear his advice, again. "Don't be afraid to live," my soul mate had said as I held his hand during the deathwatch. "The boys need you. Be strong for them." Of course, I promised him anything that I thought would bring him comfort. After his death, no matter how long the night seemed, it was never quite long enough for me to feel like facing another day. Grief weighed me down until I felt that I would crumble beneath the load, yet I knew that somehow I had to rise above my loss and begin functioning more normally or my sons would become orphans.

I collected some inexpensive comforts: a few geese, and a handful of ducklings. Hearing of my love for birds, someone gave me a few canaries; another gave me some zebra finches; someone else, a pair of diamond doves. One day I read an article about Gouldian finches and was enchanted by their brilliant colors—a living rainbow! The article said that they also had a beautiful song. If their song was anything like their color, it would be breathtaking.

Exotic birds are not easy to find in northern British Columbia, so I asked my good friend, Linda, who was raising canaries at that time, if she could find me a Gouldian.

When Linda delivered my little Rainbow, I was mesmerized. The picture I had seen didn't begin do him justice! He was a youngster, just finishing his juvenile molt, but even at that young age, the intensity of his color touched a responsive chord deep in my soul. When my sense of loss left me feeling cold and colorless, when I could do nothing else, I watched my little Rainbow. His beauty melted the hard places that seemed to be forming in my heart.

Not long after I received my Gouldian, I got a phone call late one Saturday evening in mid-January. It was my nearest neighbor calling me from a radiophone in her truck. She informed me that they were stuck in our shared driveway and wondered if I knew anyone with a skidder or grader who could pull them out. I told her that I didn't know anyone with equipment who would start it up on this very cold night. It had been unseasonably warm for over a week, but the temperature had dropped to nearly thirty degrees below zero Celsius in just a few hours.

When I asked her how she got stuck, she told me they had been emptying their sewer and that the pumping truck became stuck in the sewage. When I asked why they would be emptying their sewage onto the driveway, she became impatient with me and abruptly hung up.

Ever protective of the environment, it had bothered me to see the Peace Country I so loved subjected to the careless dumping of dangerous waste. I had heard of barrels being dumped into unnamed lakes nearby and trucks from other parts of British Columbia being seen dumping their contents onto crown land (the United States equivalent of a national forest) not far from residential areas. I had heard rumors, which later proved true, of radioactive materials being dropped down casings drilled into the earth right beside the Pine River and then being filled with cement. An earthquake, causing a realignment of the soil, would do considerable damage to the water supply. Was it now acceptable protocol to dump septic contents onto driveways?

I called the local RCMP detachment and an officer reassured me that it was illegal to dump sewage near public roads and that I should get the license number of the truck. Josh volunteered to record the license. I phoned my sister, Deb, who lived nearby, and she met Josh in the driveway. They were surprised to learn that this pumper truck was actually a huge oil field truck presently offloading a large amount of clear yellow liquid from an eight-inch hose off to the side of the driveway. It did not look or smell anything like sewage. It smelled of strong chemicals.

After they watched the unloading of the pumper truck, Deb and Josh drove over to my parents' house (a stone's throw from my house and equidistant to my neighbor's) to join Zach and me. It appeared that the truck, loaded with chemicals, came into our driveway and got stuck while attempting to empty a portion of its tank full of chemicals before it could pump out our neighbor's sewer tank. After the sewage tank was pumped, we expected to hear the truck drive away. Instead, it began pumping again. We looked at each other, all thinking the same thing.

"Surely they won't dump the sewage beside the road too!" But they did! Josh and Deb went to the dumpsite again and told the young driver not to continue dumping the contents of his truck. In not such kind words, the neighbor told Deb and Josh to leave. I met an RCMP officer shortly before midnight at the highway to show him the dump site. This was the first time I had seen the mess. There was an overpowering smell. We were both shocked when he shone his flashlight on the steaming, gray lake of what we were later told was "frac fluid." This fluid is a mixture of very strong, non-biodegradable chemicals, the combination of which depends upon what type of fractured rock is being dissolved in the drilling process. The truck should have been emptied of this "frac fluid" before being used to pump sewage. During his inspection of the liquid, he stepped into the edge of this liquid chemical. The next day his boots came apart at the seams.

On my way to work the following Friday, my car got stuck in a snowdrift beside the chemical spill. I shoveled for two hours breathing what I now know to be classified as toxic vapors. The longer I was there, the more challenging it was for me to breathe. By the time I reached the hospital for my shift, I felt very strange. Long before I returned home, I had spiraled into an indescribably intense illness.

The vapors were so strong from the "spill" that my house was filled with the odor. My little Zach became ill. We both had high fevers. My head seemed too heavy to lift from my pillow. In the morning, my pillow was spotted with blood. Zach and Josh both had bloodstained pillows as well. I coughed so hard that I lost muscle control of my bladder. My breathing sounded like puffed rice popping in a bowl of milk—snapping so loudly that the sound often interrupted my sleep.

It was five days before I could get out of bed, and then I was too weak to drive. A family member took me to the clinic. After listening to my lungs, the physician prescribed a pneumonia antibiotic. Each day was a harder struggle for breath than the day before. When I finished my third course of antibiotics, lab tests were negative for bacteria or fungus in my lungs, but the next X-ray revealed fluid in the lower portion of each lung. My blood-oxygen levels were dangerously low. No matter what the doctors tried, I did not improve. I just could not get enough oxygen.

When my doctor secured a portable oxygen unit for me, I was able to return home, though I was in constant pain. Three courses of antibiotics had wiped my digestive system clean, and I was having bowel trouble. I had also developed an intense burning sensation on my upper back, and I could not escape it no matter what sleeping position or lotion I tried. It was frustrating that no one could figure out how to treat me or discover the cause of my illness. Perhaps there was no treatment, for the odd symptoms I displayed were those which, I now know, typify a chemical burn to the lungs.

I felt like an alien, alone in the universe with a mysterious, untreatable condition. Hospitalized, even on oxygen twenty-four hours a day, I had no energy, so family and friends cared for my boys, my animals, and birds. No one really understood my pain. With my soul mate gone, my heart ached for communion. Medical personnel whom I had counted as friends began to treat me like a medical oddity. I got tired of asking questions and researching my illness, but not before I had alienated members of my immediate family and many of my friends. Seven years after my husband's death, I was admitted to the room next door to where Dave died. After a few days of treatments that brought no relief, I was sent home. I had never felt so hopeless and forsaken.

Unable to sleep, I got out of bed, picked up a writing pad and pen, sat down at the kitchen table, and began to record my physical and spiritual struggle in the form of a prayer. I could not see the page through my tears, but I was thankful to have some quiet time to relinquish my grip on life, if that was my Father's will.

I was nearly finished recording my prayer of surrender when I heard a soft trilling sound. Lifting my head, I wiped my eyes and strained to see through the darkness, my pen poised over the concluding sentence. I listened intently for a few seconds but heard nothing more.

Probably a mouse. I hate emptying traps. That was Dave's job.

Then, floating sweetly through the darkness, came the first faint notes of an enchanting melody. So delicate was the sound that I thought I was imagining or recalling a nostalgic memory. As the song intensified, I became more puzzled. The canaries never sang after sundown. My birds were always quiet at night. At last, I identified the singer. It was my little Rainbow!

I laid down my pen, leaned back in my old kitchen chair, closed my eyes, and allowed the song to envelop me. So entrancing was the sweet mixture of sounds that I lost all sense of time. It was a doxology of praise, anointing oil for my anguished soul. Gently, reverently, it massaged the ache deep within my heart until my discontent and sense of rejection disappeared. Rainbow's song was the most beautiful and healing sound I will ever hear this side of heaven. It was a cascade of liquid tones and elegant trills similar to the warble of a canary but softer, sweeter, more glorious.

Suddenly, I knew I was not alone. My written petition had received an immediate answer. I knew the all-encompassing love of God in a way I had never known it before. I have always been a believer, but the night Rainbow sang to me I knew my Father was sending me a very personalized message that He would never forsake me. At the peak of my extremity, Rainbow delivered the song of life and hope. My boys would not be orphans. Whatever happened, I was not alone.

Rainbow had never sung before, and he never sang again. He didn't need to.

His song is still with me. It has been several years since the spill, and I am still housebound, unable to catch a whiff of any chemical fumes without a serious setback. My house has been modified to accommodate my sensitivities. I am on oxygen, but I have learned to live within my restraints.

Sometimes, the nights are long. I still miss Dave, but the memory of Rainbow's song helps me highlight my blessings instead of my limitations.

Just a Little Higher

Zach finished high school, Josh is graduating from college, and I am still alive. I am never alone. But I am certain that I would not have lived if Rainbow's song had not enlightened my darkest hour.

Author's note: No one has yet been deemed responsible for the chemical spill that changed Linda's life.

A Farewell

My fairest child, I have no song to give you;
No lark could pipe to skies so dull and gray;
Yet, ere we part, one lesson I can leave you
    For every day.

Be good, sweet maid, and let who will be clever;
Do noble things, not dream them, all day long:
And so make life, death, and that vast forever
    One grand, sweet song.

—*Charles Kingsley*

Charlie's Home

Consider the ravens:
for they neither sow nor reap;
which neither have storehouse or barn;
and God feedeth them:
how much more are ye
better than the fowls?

—Luke 12:24

I had known Anne for years, but it wasn't until just a month before she moved to California that she shared with me the dark secrets of her wounded soul and the extraordinary raven who helped her heart to heal from the wounds of war.

"The man in the park told us you always take orphans!" the teenagers insisted. I looked down at the two baby ravens then back at their kidnappers. The students were in a pickle. They couldn't take the chicks to school after their field trip to Glacier Park, and their parents wouldn't want the young birds either. But that spring day, back in 1965, it was much easier to open my front door than to open my heart. I was still picking up the pieces of my shattered life.

We had been a happy family until my husband, Ron, was called away to war. When he returned from Korea, a battle still raged beneath the bronze and silver stars that were pinned over his heart. Though I was proud of his accomplishments, I couldn't help but notice uncharacteristic behavior: he couldn't sleep through the night without awakening in a cold sweat at least once, he became less able to perform simple chores without growing frustrated, and he seemed unable to control his anger. His noisy outbursts escalated with friends at work, with our five children, and with me. He seemed suspicious about everything. He would speak to no one about the war but raved night after night in his sleep about the soldiers he was unable to save. A peace-loving man, Ron had served as a medic, refusing to bear arms. Now he kept a gun in the house—loaded.

On September 30, 1955, Ron held the children and me at gunpoint for several hours. I managed to get the four oldest children out of the house and told them to run to the neighbor's. When we finally escaped, the baby and I had been badly beaten, and my clothing hung in shreds.

The police formed a manhunt in the nearby woods. I watched, with aching heart, as my once tender and loving husband was shackled like a wild beast and shoved into a patrol car to spend the next several months huddled in a dark corner of a tiny prison cell. He needed medical attention, but no one really knew what to do for him.

I begged for a hearing with a prominent judge to validate Ron's easy-going personality before he went to war and how he had degenerated to his present condition. I hoped that the judge might direct me to a specialist who could give Ron a miraculous medicine, but his verdict was anything but hopeful.

"Mrs. Lawton, your husband is exhibiting psychotic behavior that is consistent with paranoid schizophrenia," he said, not without pity. "Ron must be committed to a mental institution. I cannot guarantee that he will change much, but with proper care and consistent medication, he may improve."

My heart dropped like lead. The room spun in slow motion. Still in a daze, and with great reluctance, I signed the necessary papers, having already been assured by several professionals that it was Ron's only hope of getting better.

Charlie's Home

I visited him faithfully, hoping and praying for his healing, but he did not improve. Our conversations during my visits to the asylum were entirely one sided. Ron was totally withdrawn and seemed to have lost all interest in life. Finally, he would not even acknowledge my presence. For several years, I hovered near the hospital, spending much of my emotional and physical energy just ... hoping. I resisted considering the possibility that Ron and I would never be together again.

Meanwhile, our neighbors began treating the children and me as if we had leprosy. Parents would not allow their children to play with mine. At the elementary school where I worked, my ability to teach was closely scrutinized. There was no light, no hope that anything would change for the better.

On the day that the two raven chicks arrived at my door, it had been more than ten years since my husband's incarceration and I'd had a particularly bad day. My heart was definitely not feeling warm and fuzzy, but what chance did the two downy, orphaned ravens have if I didn't accept them? Our home, near Glacier National Park in Montana, had been unofficially declared a haven for neglected and unwanted animals, tame or wild, probably because I understood and empathized with their plight. I too was misplaced. Reluctantly, I reached out. The smaller raven failed to live, but Charlie survived.

The change that Charlie would bring to the Lawton household defied all logic.

Charlie began his career by charging through the barriers that the neighbors had erected against us. Children absolutely could not resist him. They began coming over to "Charlie's home." One little boy sat on our lawn and dug worms for over three hours one day, fascinated by Charlie's swallowing mechanism.

Next to eating worms, Charlie's favorite activity was snuggling. Our dog, Zeke, loved orphans. He'd already successfully raised a litter of abandoned kittens and twelve mallard ducklings that year. Zeke had no orphans when Charlie arrived, so it was he who supplied most of the cuddling that the downy chick desired. Charlie filled Zeke's obsession to feel needed. It was comical to watch the chick endure the bath that the dog insisted on delivering before he would snuggle with the gangly, half-naked chick. Charlie would close his eyes, in either resignation or ecstasy, and sit as still as he could in spite of being raised off the ground with every swipe of Zeke's parental tongue.

Like good seed in broken soil, my wounded heart gradually opened to Charlie's warmth and humor. On Ron's final home visit, he had refused his medication, and it ended in the usual disaster. It was to little Charlie that I finally admitted the reality of my husband's permanent absence. Charlie's steady exuberance, and his ability to adapt, helped me quit looking back so often. My broken heart began to heal.

Breaking the Spell

Charlie was always happy. In spite of having been stolen from his nest and adopted by aliens, he refused to discern anything but pleasure in circumstances. Iridescence settled onto his pre-adult plumage, and it seemed that he left me with a little piece of rainbow after every snuggling session. Where once there had been only blackness, I began to discern glimpses of color. I don't know exactly how he accomplished it, but before he was fully grown, I preferred looking at life through Charlie's eyes.

When Charlie first came, I could see neighbors peeking out from behind their curtains whenever our family walked through the neighborhood. It was against my nature to accept the suspicious stares of those who didn't trust the legendary harbinger of evil who lived with us. I could just imagine what they were thinking; I was the wife of a man who lived in an insane asylum and my best friend was a big, black raven that rode on my shoulder. Like something from a horror script, they seemed to suspect that I could cast an evil spell by muttering a few unintelligible words at some unsuspecting passerby. At first, I resented Charlie for the stereotype with which he abeled the Lawton family, but I learned that what appears to be a curse can be a blessing. The outcome depends on how you allow yourself to look at it.

Because we fed Charlie worms by digging for them with a hoe, our orphan deduced that anyone with a hoe in hand should supply him with a meal. If no worms were immediately forthcoming, Charlie would remind the digger, with a painful peck on the foot, that he was waiting. I feared that his insistent attitude would add to the sense of foreboding, but most everyone shared a treat with him from the garden or the cupboard. Smiles reappeared around our neighborhood. Everybody knew and loved Charlie.

As he matured, Charlie expected doors to open for him, and so they did. He learned to ask for what he wanted. Who could resist a talking bird? He would tap at the front door, wait for it to open, and then say a cordial, "Hello there!" to anyone who answered his knock. He was generally greeted with, "Hi there, Charlie!" a smile, a pat on the head, and a treat.

Never a day went by that I didn't have a good laugh at some trick Charlie played on the kids, the dog, the cats, the chickens, or sometimes even the horse. With age, Charlie's genius sharpened. After he learned to talk, he would use his imitation of my voice to call his surrogate father to the back porch: "Zeke ... Zeke!" The dog would rip around the corner of the house only to discover his bowl empty *again*. Charlie would fly to the top of a tree and laugh his loud and raucous rendition of a belly laugh. Zeke would ignore Charlie the rest of the day, the worst punishment our gregarious bird could suffer.

O Canada!

My physical and emotional health had been in a steady decline due to the emotional strain of Ron's illness. I was finally encouraged by my physicians to move to another location, away from the facility in which Ron was incarcerated. It was not long after Charlie reached adulthood that I accepted a teaching position in Chetwynd, British Columbia. The children were excited to be going to Canada. We packed a few belongings into a trailer, loaded Charlie into his travel cage—an old orange crate—and headed north.

At the Canadian border crossing, the customs officers appeared not to notice Charlie in spite of his insistent, "Hi there! Hi there!" from the back seat. I have no idea how many laws we broke bringing Charlie into Canada—nor do I know what we would have done if Charlie had been denied entrance—but he helped save at least one life by being allowed to cross the border.

At a rest stop in the Kootenays, just outside of Golden, British Columbia, we stopped for a picnic lunch on our way north. Charlie acted upset when we let him out for exercise. A poodle standing guard over an infant in a car seat at the neighboring table suddenly began barking toward the bushes. Seconds later, a mountain lion ran into our midst, grabbed the dog, and was back in the bushes before anyone could utter a cry! Charlie flew above that devil cat, faithfully reporting his position to anyone who would listen. Following his lead, the authorities found the dangerous animal who had little or no fear of humans.

Charlie adapted to the north as if he'd been born there. Children of the Cree Nation in my class at Don Titus Elementary School in Chetwynd, British Columbia, attributed magical powers to him; here was their own sacred bird, free to go wherever he wanted, yet he chose to live among humans! Many of us were held under Charlie's spell—including one reluctant veterinarian.

Broken Leg

Upon returning home from school one day, I discovered Charlie squatting on the lawn. He did not fly to me as usual. I knelt beside him and lifted him as gently as I could. What I discovered made me nauseous. One leg dangled at an odd angle, obviously broken. Though funds were tight, I took him to the only vet who would consent to see him, over 150 kilometers

Charlie's Home

(ninety miles) away in Fort St. John. The vet was doubtful about Charlie's recovery.

"I'm sorry, Mrs. Lawton, but I think it would be best to put him out of his misery."

Five anxious pairs of eyes were lined up around the examination table pleading with the doctor, silently but intently, to spare the life of their friend. I begged him to try something—anything. The vet seemed more concerned about the damage that Charlie's monstrous beak might inflict than about his broken leg. He suggested a muzzle, but I told him Charlie would never hurt anyone. He shrugged and shook his head as if he'd heard that story once too often. While Charlie nestled in my arms, the good doctor quickly taped a couple of tongue depressors to the broken limb. Charlie endured the pain like a good soldier. I fumbled in my purse for some cash, but the vet smiled and waved his hand.

"Charlie is the most remarkable animal I have ever treated!" He smiled. "I couldn't think of charging you! Charlie was my entertainment for today!"

"Thank you, kind sir," I whispered past the lump in my throat.

After he broke his leg, Charlie became more dependent upon flight. I worried that someday he would choose to fly away and join his wild cousins. No one in the Lawton family enjoyed visiting more than Charlie. I knew he must be wandering afar, for he would often swoop into the yard and land on the hood of my old Rambler just as we returned from school. Sometimes he wasn't home as we arrived. He would fly into the yard shortly thereafter, and I would hear the children's familiar cry as they ran to the door.

"Charlie's home!"

If I happened to be outside when he returned, Charlie would fly to my shoulder and I would listen while he, with his vocabulary of about twenty-five words, would tell me about his day. I would tell him how beautiful he was and how much we had missed him, then he would fly to the top of a nearby spruce tree and watch over his family, like a forest monarch, until daybreak.

The Entertainer

Because of his broken leg, Charlie developed a permanent limp. He used it to his advantage when he entertained, and he entertained regularly—or maybe *irregularly* would more accurately describe his antics. Next to our own yard, Charlie spent more time at East Pine Service Station than anywhere else. It had just the right combination of food and fun. The local people referred to the small service station as East Pine Park. It wasn't many miles from our house, as the raven flies. It consisted of a gas station, a convenience store, and a few picnic tables. Tourists on their way up the Alaska Highway, stopping for gas and refreshments, were more than a little startled at Charlie's friendliness. He invented all sorts of amusing tricks. He would stretch his neck out, lay his head on his back, look (upside-down) at the people behind him and make a hollow, honking noise. Then, leaning forward, he would put his head between his legs and clack his huge beak. People were naturally drawn to him, and Charlie listened intently to anyone who spoke to him. Cocking his head from side to side, he would try to repeat their words.

Charlie had been with us just over six years when I received a telephone call from a man in Nebraska. The man had played detective until he finally found our telephone number.

"I'd like to buy your trained raven, ma'am," he said. "I haven't been able to get him out of my mind since I left East Pine. That bird talked as if he knew what he was saying! I'm prepared to give you $175 for him."

His offer did not tempt me, though I could have used the money. "I'm sorry, sir, but I can't sell Charlie."

"I can pay more," he assured me. "Name your price!"

"No, sir. I can't sell him. He's not mine to sell."

"Oh ... then who should I call?"

"Nobody. He's free."

"Free ... ?" A long silence followed. In my mind's eye, I pictured the man ready to drop the receiver and head for Canada to pick up a very economical investment.

Struggling to find words to describe our bond, I stole a glance out the kitchen window. Charlie was pestering the dog—again. Zeke had a rock collection that he had acquired through the years. Whenever we went on a picnic, Zeke never failed to bring home one special rock to add to his stash, and though he was mild-mannered about everything else, no one dared touch his collection of gemstones. Charlie was taunting the old dog into playing catch-me-if-you-can. I smiled as I watched Charlie very slowly and deliberately step across the lawn toward Zeke's pile of rocks, glancing intermittently back at the dog who was watching his every move.

I knew the game well. It was one Zeke couldn't refuse. Charlie would finally stretch his neck out toward one particular rock. That was Zeke's cue to growl viciously and make a mad dash toward Charlie, as if to tear the bird wing from wing. As usual, Charlie rose to a low-hanging branch, just out of reach of the dog's vicious teeth. Then Charlie would open his beak wide in a hearty belly laugh. This display of rivalry was mere entertainment. The two animals were devoted to each other. I smiled first at Charlie and then at my pitiful attempt to make this man from Nebraska understand something that even I couldn't grasp. Why *did* Charlie stay with us?

"Well, sir, he's ... he's ... just Charlie. He goes where he pleases, and it pleases him to be with us. I don't know what we'd do without him! Thank you for calling."

Charlie's Rainbows

Shortly after Charlie turned nine, he did not alight on the hood of my old Rambler when I returned home from school one spring day. That was unusual. I scanned the horizon. At last, I found him crumpled on the front porch, his beautiful, black breast pierced by a pellet. Cradling him in my arms, I recalled that he came to me when I had decided not to care anymore. I was tired of crying, and tired of trying, but he had needed me so desperately. When had we reversed rolls? I couldn't remember the exact day, I only knew that it was because of Charlie that I, eventually, began to care about living.

I smiled through my tears as I remembered the day that my children had taught an awkward fledgling to fly by repeatedly pushing him off the windowsill. I heard Charlie's laughter, his cheerful, "Hello!" Never again would he tap at my door and ask, "Corn?" I pressed my lips to his silent beak, then ran my fingers over his once broken leg. It had healed. Would I? The little lump in his leg felt like an invitation.

Awe and emptiness, like ravishing sea waves, took turns washing over me. What would I do without Charlie? We had needed each other. We had lifted each other. Charlie knew I would have searched the earth for him, and, in his dying effort, he returned home.

As I sat there on my front steps with Charlie in my lap, I smoothed the rainbows hidden in his shiny feathers. A tear fell, beaded up, and rolled into my lap. I smiled at the metaphor; how like Charlie to spurn my sorrow!

A piece of my soul lies buried under a big cottonwood in the Peace Country of northern British Columbia. Statistics say that Charlie lived as long as most wild ravens, but no amount of time with him could have prepared me for the great vacancy of his absence. His death tempted me to magnify the injustices of life. My children moped for weeks. Old Zeke lay beside his rock collection hour after hour, one eye on the horizon, hoping for one more game of catch-me-if-you-can. He jerked to attention whenever a raven soared through Charlie's no-fly zone.

Charlie had come to me when life could get no darker, bringing with him my daily dose of sunshine. As a tribute to his memory, and in response to the last invitation of my dusky benefactor, I decided to focus on the rainbows instead of the rain. I'd been a slow learner, but among his many virtues, Charlie was a good teacher.

Charlie's Home—Forevermore!

(Apologies to Edgar Allen!)

In my dreams, I sometimes wander to my mansion waiting yonder,
Dreaming dreams no mortal ever dared to dream before.
All my family gathered 'round me, glittering mansion to surround me,
Unknown pleasures to astound me—seems
I couldn't possibly want more.
Then the Lord of all creation interrupts my meditation
With a gem from heaven's store.

Suddenly there comes a tapping, as of someone gently rapping.
So familiar is the tapping that we turn toward the door.
All my soul within me burning, all my gold and silver spurning,
Quickly from my treasures turning, memory stirs me to the core.
For I hear nostalgic rapping, as from distant, earthen shore.
"Could it be? Forevermore!"

"Charlie's home!" the children chorus.
"He must have been looking for us!"
Here I rise to greet the stranger tapping at my mansion door.
Statue, stunned, astonished am I, standing stone-like at the door.
"Do my immortal eyes deceive me? Is this specter sent to grieve me?
Surely, you will have to leave me as you had to do before?"
Quoth my raven, "Nevermore!"

Black and glossy, just as saucy as he was in days of yore—
My immortal soul beguiling, human heart within me riling,
Charlie, flying, crying, smiling, nestles in my arms once more!
"Charlie, friend, how I have missed you!
In my dreams how oft I've kissed you!
He, himself, could not resist you, as you tapped at heaven's door!"
Quoth the raven, "Nevermore …

"No more tears and no more crying, no
more sadness, no more sighing.
No more death or hate or hunger, pain or war."
Charlie's words so softly spoken, leg so straight as never broken,
From the Lord Himself a token of the sacred love He bore.
Love felt He for human treasure, love beyond His pain or pleasure;
Love of God without a measure, sending Charlie to our door
To be parted—nevermore.

—Linda Franklin

Kiwi

There is no fear in love; but perfect love casteth out fear: because fear hath torment. He that feareth is not made perfect in love.

—1 John 4:18

I had known Lou for over twenty years before I clued in on her dark secret. She—range rider, rifleman, ranch hand, rough-and-tumble country mom—was afraid of birds! What could be done to help her? Was there some kind of healing therapy available? All it took, was one special little bird with an energetic love of singing, and Lou's crippling fear was miraculously replaced by love.

"I hate birds!" Lou shudders involuntarily, closes her eyes, and shakes her head when I invite her into my aviary. "Can't stand the fluttering! It's the only thing I am afraid of, Linda!" Her frown softens as a cascade of melody drifts into the living room.

"Oh, but I do love how your canaries sing!" Her mischievous grin reappears.

"Wouldn't you like to just look at them?" I ask, knowing how unfair it is that fear has blinded her to beauty. "They are all in cages. They won't fly at you."

Reluctantly, she follows me toward the large room where I spend the first hour of my day. The lack of pigment in our long, northern winters first sparked my interest in their bright colors, but it was the richness of their song and the unique characteristics of each bird that captured my heart. I named them for their character traits: Faith, Freedom, Trust, Jewel, Majesty, Peace, Liberty, Joy, and many more.

I ache to share my wonder with Lou, a highly respected citizen in our little village in the North Peace. Her fear is out of character with the courage she consistently displays in the face of danger at Foot Hills Ranch, where she and her husband, Jack, raised their three children: Dianne, Avis, and Tim. Never keeping their blessings to themselves, Lou leads her family to the aid of those in need of clothing, blankets, and food. For many years Lou was our community services director, packing food hampers for the hungry and boxing up clean, used clothing for disaster and famine relief shipments overseas. Having seen her own dream house, a beautiful log home, destroyed by fire, Lou never fails to share a big dose of hope with those who fear that their world has ended.

Lou brings a song with her wherever she goes. Every fundraiser in the Jackfish Community Hall, any cause from birthing to burnout, finds her expertly fingering her twelve-string guitar to the complicated melody of "Tennessee Flat Top Box" and other selections from her grand collection of old country songs. Then she closes with a hymn: "I'll Fly Away," "Over the Sunset Mountains," or "Some Wonderful Day."

Lou can't help singing. She and her siblings have an inborn talent for music. Lou's mother gave her a few piano lessons as a child, and then she taught herself to play guitar, violin, mandolin, banjo, Dobro, and mouth harp.

Lou has faced wolves and grizzlies in protecting her assortment of youngsters, including four grandchildren who consider Foothills Ranch the best place in the whole world to spend their summer holidays. They all have a love for the great outdoors, its beauty, and its creatures, and they are capable ranch hands. Life has had its share of setbacks, but through triumph and tragedy, Lou sings. It is so out of character for her to be frightened by a bird that, as we approach my aviary, I have to ask why.

"I don't know," she says as she frowns. "My earliest memory is the fear of feathers! If ever Mamma wanted me to stay downstairs, all she had to do was place a single feather on the bottom step of the staircase!" Lou peeks cautiously through the doorway of my aviary. "I've been afraid of feathers and birds for as long as I can remember."

Lou steps slowly into the aviary, as if she expects the floor to swallow her. When a few of the fledglings in the big flight cage fly upward at her approach, Lou gasps and raises her arm to cover her eyes, the same motion she would use to protect herself from a flash of fire.

I place my hand gently on her shoulder. "Lou, if you had a bird, maybe your fear would diminish," I suggest.

"Nope. Don't want a bird," she says, and walks swiftly out of the room.

A few weeks later, the phone rings.

"Linda, I'm ready to bring my singer home!" Lou says.

You could've knocked me over with a feather! Yearning to choose the perfect bird, I step into my sanctuary, carefully considering each mature male for color, song, and personality. I finally settle on a green and yellow variegated cock that I had planned to keep in order to expand my breeding program, but I can spare him. I'll have to—he is singing his heart out! I groom his nails, bathe and blow-dry him, and place him in a single cage where he continues his song in spite of his change of environment. Adaptable too. That's good.

On March 24, 1996, Lou picks up her singer. I warn her that it generally takes some time, perhaps a couple of weeks, for the bird to begin singing in new surroundings.

That evening, as she and Jack begin their usual evening worship, Lou reaches for her twelve-string and begins to sing a vesper hymn. That little bird fairly bursts with praise! There are tears of joy in Lou's voice when she calls me that evening.

"He's absolutely perfect, Linda," Lou says excitedly. "Thanks so much!"

When Dianne's twins, Katie and Jackie, arrive for their summer at the ranch, they both fall in love with Grandma's canary.

"What's his name, Gram?" Katie asks.

"I guess you can name him for me, girls!"

It didn't take them more than a couple of minutes. "His name is Kiwi, Gram," says Jackie.

Every evening, Kiwi heartily joins in their sunset songs. Together their spirits soar to their home "somewhere beyond the blue," as Grandma Lou paints radiant song pictures of the mansions awaiting them. The girls often request "Dear Jesus," a song Lou wrote about her own experience.

Dear Jesus

I was blind, I could not see,
I stumbled, Lord, away from Thee,
But your loving arms, they pulled me back to you.
You held me close to you in love,
Dear Son of God, from up above, And without you,
I know that I would fail.

Chorus:
Dear Jesus, I love you!
You've forgiven me so much
And I know
That is why I love you so.

So many times I fell away,
And then, "Forgive me, Lord," I'd pray.
And you were always willing to take me back again.
I don't deserve your love for me,
But I know you'll give it free.
What a wonderful Savior you are!

Kiwi

> Even though I've hurt you so,
> You never turned away, oh, no!
> You just hold me closer in your loving arms.
> And when this battle on earth is done,
> And the victory is won,
> I'll be with you because of your love.

A few months later, Lou begins having problems swallowing, then walking, then she develops a weakness in her hands and is no longer able to paint scenes of the Peace Country she so loves. After being diagnosed with ALS, Lou Gehrig's disease, she lays down her guitar for the last time. When I learn the devastating news, I ask her for a tape of some of her favorite cowboy hymns because I want to be able to remember her voice. Secretly, I hope that Kiwi might be singing along with her.

As I ease into the pew beside her one Sabbath, Lou's gentle smile and soft brown eyes are more beautiful than ever. Since she can no longer speak, she painstakingly writes me a note on her erasable board: "Glad to see you." Then, with careful deliberation, she hands me her homemade tape with a note taped on it: "I had to take some songs off of practice tapes, so there are some mistakes."

The service over, Lou leaves the sanctuary, leaning heavily on Jack's strong arm. He slows his pace to support his beloved. Though I haven't yet listened to the tape, I can, as I watch them walking together down the long hallway, hear the *old* Lou singing the last song I'd heard her sing in church about not being able to walk with Him holding her hand.

On the way home, I play the tape. The first notes I hear are not Lou but little Kiwi. He introduces the song and then sings along with Lou as if he knew that her melodies would have been incomplete without him. The harmonies are more touching than either of them could have achieved while singing alone. I don't know I am crying until I roll down the window and the breeze evaporates my tears. I can't decide if this pain I feel is extreme grief or deep joy. What I do know is that it has something to do with the story behind the song Lou writes and sings.

Just a Little Higher

> Now Jesus is my life, my all in all.
> Praise God the day that I had heard His call,
> With Him I have no fear of death,
> He cast my sin from east to west.
> Still He says He'll help me if I fall.

It has only been a few weeks since her church family modified the back entrance of the church because Lou *did* fall. The disease is advancing rapidly. She was alone the day she fell—or was she? If you ask, she'll confirm her strong belief with a song: "He says He'll help me if I fall." By now, the wind is unable to keep up with my flow of tears as song after song assures me of Lou's hope beyond the grave.

> Down here in this world where I'm just a pilgrim,
> Many times things don't go like I plan.
> But whatever comes, I'm trusting in Jesus,
> And He is holding my life in His hands.

I know that she believes in the words she and Kiwi are asking me about where I will be a million years from now, and it's not difficult for me to picture where Lou might be: under a tree, strumming a shiny instrument with golden strings while a little, green-and-yellow bird perches nearby to harmonize.

I cannot see the tears Lou sheds in secret as she prepares to bid her loved ones farewell a little sooner than she had planned. One thing I do know is that her eyes register no panic or apprehension. Little Kiwi's love songs seem to have gently, and completely, healed her fears.

Kiwi and Lou have both gone to their rest, but they still sing to me from my precious homemade tape, mistakes and all! So precisely does Kiwi bridge and harmonize, it's as if his voice had been accentuated, edited, and dubbed from a prerecorded session. Even before the first chords are strummed, as if in great anticipation of the absolute joy for which he was

Kiwi

destined, Kiwi is warbling an introduction to Lou's theme song. Everyone in Lou's little valley, nestled in the foothills of the Rocky Mountains, has heard her sing the song about going home, some wonderful day.

Even before that wonderful day comes, *someone* revealed a secret to my friend Lou. He told her that fear is a torment and that perfect love can cast it out. Kiwi delivered the same message to Lou that angels have shared down through the ages, "Be not afraid." Who would have thought that Lou's fear could be so easily replaced with something as simple and as miraculous as a song?

When Linda read this story to Lou, she nodded her head in approval, wept silently for a minute or two, and then laboriously wrote her final note to Linda: "I wish I still had him." Lou passed to her rest a month after this story was written.

Overheard in an Orchard

Said the Robin to the Sparrow,
"I should really like to know
Why these anxious human beings
Rush about and worry so."

Said the Sparrow to the Robin,
"Friend, I think that it might be
That they have no heavenly Father
Such as cares for you and me."

—*Elizabeth Cheney*

Once Upon a Song

*If you keep a green bough within your heart,
there will come one day, to stay, a singing bird.*

—Onitsura

Her entire world had caved in, and JoAnn's pain was draining the life out of her. Nothing, it seemed, could break her free-fall into despondency. Who knows what might have happened, had it not been for a child's love for one tiny, injured chick? He was just a plain, brown bird, but his little heart held the secret of true joy, and he was willing to share it.

I was having a hard time coping with the miserable hand life had dealt. I was abandoned, confused, and discouraged. The only encouraging thought I could think was that he would surely come back and apologize to the kids and me. Then it would come clear, or at least I would try to understand. During those early days, with our family broken, happiness was a distant memory. Fear and anger threatened to defeat me.

I was visiting a friend and her family when I realized that I hadn't heard the children's voices for a while. I am sure that my face registered all the panic I was feeling.

"Vickie!" I asked breathlessly. "Do you know where the kids are?"

"Yes, they are all down at the park, JoAnn." She laid her hand on my arm and looked into my eyes. "The children are safe. Are you all right?"

Just a Little Higher

I needed reassurance that I was still a good mother. As I neared the park, my youngest—four-year-old Freddy—ran to me with something cupped in his little hands.

"Mamma, Mamma! Look what I found!" Freddy was breathless with excitement.

As the other children gathered around us, Freddy dumped a slobbery little ball of fuzz into my hand. It was the sorriest excuse for a bird I had ever seen. All of the children began talking at once while I tried to piece the story together. Apparently, a neighborhood dog had destroyed a nest of chicks on a low-hanging branch and Freddy had rescued this one. But to what end? Surely the chick would die. It was so tiny. Its eyes were barely open. Carefully spreading the sparse chest feathers, I discovered a puncture wound in his breast. There was really no hope.

If I'd had any tears left, I sure wouldn't waste them on a bird. I couldn't cope with another loss. I didn't want to cry anymore. Still ...

I looked past the chick and into the trusting eyes of my little one. Freddy was always coming to the rescue of some unfortunate creature. He was a magnet for orphans of every description. I never knew what he would bring home next. I'd do just about anything to preserve his trust. He was too young, still too full of hope.

"You can save him, can't you, Mamma? I told 'em you could!" Freddy bragged.

Five pairs of eyes were looking at me. Five pairs of ears were listening for a word of hope. None of them were even moving. They were just ... waiting ... expecting. Freddie's trust was complete.

I looked down at the little chick, as if it held the answer. It snuggled down into my hand. I smiled at Freddy, cradled the injured fledgling close to my heart, and headed back to Vickie's house with all five youngsters behind me, skipping and turning cartwheels of joy. I felt like a mother quail heading to her nest.

We cut short our visit and returned home. I crumbled some whole wheat bread into a teaspoon of milk and was pleasantly surprised when the chick gobbled it down. My hands seemed too large to feed such a tiny creature, but I was encouraged by his appetite. When he had eaten a few crumbs, I wiped his beak and placed him in the shoebox I had instructed the children to pad with a clean washcloth. Then I looked for some peroxide and sterile cotton swabs. His wound looked bad; it was a pretty deep puncture.

I'm sure I must have looked discouraged after I inspected and treated the wound, but little Fred knew what to do. With the seriousness of a minister, he announced to his sister, Shauna, and older brother, Eddy Joe, "Now, we all need to pray that he will get well."

We all knelt together around the little shoebox while Freddy prayed. "Dear Jesus, thank you for sending us this little birdie. Please help him get better soon. Amen."

The prayers that followed were somewhat repetitive, but there was no doubt about each child's sincerity. My faith was nonexistent, but the children were confident. The chick blinked up at his benefactors as if he felt right at home and expected to be well in no time.

As the children prepared for bed, I fed the chick his second meal. He snuggled into his washcloth and closed his eyes contentedly. I told the children that they should be good examples and go to sleep very quietly so as not to awaken him. Motherhood is good practice for raising a chick. Whenever he rustled in the night, I fed him, and he went right back to sleep.

Morning came much too soon. It was disgustingly bright, one of those mornings when I would have preferred to sleep all day, but Freddy was shaking me.

"His name is Tibby, Mamma," he announced. "He's gonna stay with us for a long, long time."

In spite of my doubts, Tibby kept eating and growing. I bought a birdcage at an auction. After a few comical blunders, he mastered the swing. It soon became his favorite perch. The children prayed every night. As Tibby prospered, so did my faith.

What kind of a bird was he? Someone told me that he was a "wild canary." I hoped he would eventually display some sort of color pattern so that I could identify him, but he never developed any distinguishing marks. He was just a plain, brown bird, as near as I could tell.

Before he could eat on his own, it was time for our family to move. I had thought, because he was maturing so rapidly, that I might be able to release him near Vickie's yard before we left, but he was still dependent on my bread and milk formula, so he traveled with us several hundred miles northward.

In our new home, life revolved around Tibby. He became my icon of hope ... a good omen ... a phoenix rising from the ashes of life. Long after he could take care of himself, I found myself checking on him, feeling a motherly concern. He was always happy to eat from my hand; grapes were his favorite, but he also enjoyed corn, fresh broccoli, and lettuce. The children checked in with him as soon as they came home from school and always asked for a report about what Tibby had been up to during their absence. Little Tibby was happy no matter what happened. His message came a little clearer to me every day: why choose misery when you can be happy?

Tibby was, at first, an obligation. As he matured, he became less of a burden. But when he started singing, it was I who was in his debt. Every evening as we gathered in the living room for story time and music, Tibby made his presence known. By six months of age, he was singing like the canary we had decided he must be. Although I could not find "wild canary" listed in my bird book, his song echoed those famous singers bred specifically for song. Perhaps a pair of canaries had escaped from an aviary and tried to rear their brood out of doors.

Tibby encouraged the children to practice their music. It was more fun to play the piano when a bird sang with them. (Freddy became an accomplished musician and now teaches college-level music.)

Now that Tibby was far beyond his natural climate, I knew that he would not survive the rigors of the Arctic influences. Besides, whenever I considered life without him, I felt empty inside. He stayed where I knew he would be safe: right in front of the living room window, keeping track of everything that happened. Tibby was my confidant. When no one understood my sorrow, I shared my woes with him. His advice was always the same: "Sing and play, JoAnn!"

Except for our evening gatherings around the family Bible, I had abandoned my music. Tibby drew me back to the piano. Whenever I played, he sang. I loved to hear him sing, so I kept playing. It seemed like a frivolous indulgence when my heart was so full of pain, but Tibby's insistent cheerfulness shamed me into attempting to rise above my discouragement. If anyone had a reason to be bitter, it was he. His whole family was dead. Murdered. Yet it never occurred to him to be unhappy.

It was as if Tibby was my personal gift from Eden, coming from some far away time, before joyful innocence was sacrificed to the knowledge of evil. His was no half-hearted song. He sang lustily, leaning forward on his swing, his throat fairly bursting with what I interpreted to mean, "Look on the sunny side. There are gardens to plant, books to read, songs to sing. Life is good. Don't worry, be happy!" Tibby's happy little heart had no room for sadness. His song began to lift me above the sense of uselessness that had accompanied my despair. My heart was lighter.

Pounding out those favorite old hymns on my piano, I lost track of time. As my fingers followed Tibby's lead, my heart warmed. I still sing one song in particular that I played during those first dark days. It was about keeping a song in my heart, even in the night. I played and sang it over and over again. Tibby always sang it with me.

Tibby lived with us for twelve rewarding years. And he sang every single day. He even sang the night before he died.

My children all have families of their own now. I am still in Tibby's debt. When that old, familiar feeling of rejection overwhelms me, I have only to sit myself down at the piano, close my eyes, and listen. I can always, very clearly—as if he were right above me—hear Tibby singing. His song was "a chord of hope" sent from heaven to lift a lonely heart. When death seemed preferable to life, I reached out to a helpless little bird—and then he helped me—once upon a song.

The Gulls

Soaring high
In the stormy sky
As dawn begins to gleam,
I see the birds,
And fail for words,
As they rise above the stream.

Their lonely wail
Drifts o'er the gale
Announcing the passing night.
Their idle wings,
In silence bring
Uplift to their maiden flight.

Wings angle soft,
Then reach aloft,
Where sunbeams of the dawn,
In brilliant rest
Upon their breast
Twinkle them off and on.

—*Linda Franklin*

Pigeon Toes

Oh that I had wings like a dove!
For then I would fly away, and be at rest.

—Psalm 55:6

Jed had survived his brush with death, but the burn accident had left our son terribly scarred. Could he survive his upcoming teen years without becoming bitter? How many times would I yet ask myself, "What good thing can possibly come from such a tragedy?" The day Jed introduced me to a certain pigeon, my doubts took wing.

"Hey, Mom!" Jed called to me, "That bird needs help! Think I can catch him?"

My ten-year-old son stopped tossing bread crumbs to the flock of pigeons that surrounded him when he discovered one that appeared to be crippled. Jed loved all animals, but birds had always received his special attention, especially a bird in need. Before he was six years old, he had successfully raised a very young cedar waxwing and rescued a mockingbird fledgling from certain death on the highway. Then, at the tender age of eight, Jed was trapped in an inferno that left him with severe burns over nearly half of his body, and he was suddenly the one in need.

By a unique series of miracles, Jed's life was spared. Through three long years of surgeries, countless checkups in US and Canadian burn clinics, he had maintained a cheerful spirit. For his sake, I tried to hide my tears, but I was on an emotional roller coaster.

I repeatedly asked myself, "Why did this awful thing happen to my little boy?" Then, as I witnessed more severely damaged burn survivors in hospitals and burn clinics, I secretly declared, "I am so thankful that this is *all* that happened to Jed." I tried desperately to be brave, but somewhere between the strain of flashbacks and medical appointments, my smile would begin to wobble. Whenever Jed saw this happen, he would gently touch my arm and encourage me.

"Don't cry, Mom," his blue eyes would sparkle as he looked up at me. "Everything works!"

Every six weeks, leaving Jed's father and his beloved dog behind, we traveled from our home in British Columbia's Peace Country down to Vancouver for surgeries and check-ups. Jed's progress was monitored with an ongoing series of photos taken by his plastic surgeon. He endured grueling orthodontic adjustments. He was assigned numerous therapies and splints designed to prevent muscular atrophy. He was fitted with customized pressure garments for his legs and hands to prevent his scars from thickening. We were thankful for sponsors to help us with travel expenses, but getting to appointments on time, finding parking spaces, and weighing the advice of various health professionals, was exhausting.

Jed was a country boy. The confinement of the city was harder for him to endure than his medical assignments, but he did his best to remain positive. I introduced as many simple pleasures as possible during our trips to the lower mainland. We played the story tapes parents that my parents recorded for Jed: *Where the Red Fern Grows, Summer of the Monkeys, Midnight and Jeremiah, Summer Lightning,* and *Sarah, Plain and Tall.*

This particular time, we had enjoyed listening to their newest series, *I Can Jump Puddles,* a book by Alan Marshall, an Australian lad who lost the use of his legs at age six because of polio. At the end of the story, Alan is moving to Melbourne to take an accounting course, far from his country home and his best friend, Joe.

"I wonder how you'll get on with your crutches down there," Joe mused.

"Crutches!" Alan exclaimed, dismissing the inference with contempt. "Crutches are nothing!"

Alan's wild adventures and disdain of sympathy impressed Jed. It seemed to me that he held his head just a little higher that evening as we carried our luggage into Easter Seal House, our home away from home.

The next day's schedule was even more exhausting than usual, but Jed's compensation for endurance was not an expensive gift or an exotic meal. All he wanted was some day-old bread and a visit to Granville Island; a paradise of fresh produce, book stores, coffee shops, restaurants, dessert bars, delicatessens, bakeries, art stores, and toyshops. With the relief of having our appointments behind us, we ordered a pair of fresh croissant sandwiches at the Island deli, plump with garden ripe tomatoes and crisp alfalfa sprouts, and then found a bench overlooking English Bay where we could watch the boats as we ate a late lunch. Jed finished quickly so that he could get to the main attraction; feeding the pigeons.

He discovered the crippled bird and walked back to me before he finished distributing his loaf. "See that one over there?" Jed pointed toward the rear the flock. "He's limping. There's some string and tar stuck on his feet. That bird needs help! Think I could catch him?"

"I don't know, Jed," I answered doubtfully. "He can probably still fly."

He left his bread with me and tried to catch the injured bird, but the pigeon managed to stay just out of reach. Though he returned in less than a minute, Jed did not appear defeated.

"Let's go to the Toy Factory," he urged as I finished eating. "I think I can find what I need over there." Bypassing tempting displays of kites, trains, games, and scientific models, Jed walked directly to a display case filled with butterfly nets. He paid for his purchase with birthday money that he had saved. Then, with scarcely a limp, he hurried back to the flock. Onlookers exchanged frowns while Jed eagerly sought his prize. *Who is this masked child darting in and out among our pigeons?*

Just a Little Higher

Ignoring the stares to which he was almost accustomed after nearly two years of wearing his pressure mask, Jed captured his prize. Fish line was not only wrapped around the pigeon's legs and toes, it was embedded in the flesh. The bird's feet were red, swollen, and smeared with fresh tar. Wiping the tarry feet with my napkin, I saw that one toe was missing, and two others dangled uselessly, far past saving but too firmly attached for me to remove easily. The mess would require some sort of surgical procedure. I sighed, more worried about how I would remove the tar that Jed had just smeared on the new pressure gloves he had received that day than in how I could help his new friend.

Jed's only concern was for his patient. "Mom, do you think it would be okay with Brian and Elizabeth if we take him to Easter Seal House and clean him up?"

Jed continued with a concern born in the debriding tank. "He might die if his feet get infected."

We drove back to Easter Seal House with Jed firmly holding the bird that I had christened Pigeon Toes. Keeping the bird's tarry feet in the empty bread bag, Jed comforted PT with the same consolations he had heard that very day in the VGH therapy department when Joanne and Jennifer had poured a new mold of his face while he breathed through straws (that made his nose bleed) while his face was covered with plaster for several long minutes. His new mask, created from that mold, would apply more customized pressure to his ever-thickening scars. I smiled to myself as I heard the familiar phrases.

"You're doing just fine!" Jed encouraged the frightened bird. "This procedure won't take long. We'll soon be done and you can go home. Just a small repair job. It might hurt a little, but don't panic!" (How many times had Jed diverted my panic attacks with that last phrase?) PT cocked his head, then closed his eyes and nestled down quietly in Jed's lap.

Brian, the manager at Easter Seal House, was folding sheets in the laundry room when we came into the basement from the underground parking area. Jed held the bird up to him for inspection. "Oh, *de poor liddel t'ing!"* Brian exclaimed in his enchanting South African accent. "Let's go down *de cor-r-ridor-r to de udda sink."* He donated a clean towel, a pair of nurses' scissors, some soap, and privacy to Jed's rescue project.

I attempted to lather up some courage as I washed my hands. Jed held the pigeon while I snipped the thick, tough fish line and slid it sideways, out through the flesh, much like unthreading a needle. Still lacking the nerve that I knew I would need in order to remove the pigeon's toes, I glanced doubtfully at my son.

He was restraining PT in much the same way I had steadied his own leg a few weeks earlier while the plastic surgeon peeled a strip of skin from his leg to patch the spot on his right cheek where a portion of fresh graft had been rejected. Jed opted not to have local anesthetic for the "small repair job", so the doctor performed the procedure at his bedside a mere two days after back-to-back major surgeries in which the entire lower half of Jed's face was replaced with skin harvested from his scalp. I had felt like a traitor that day, steadying my son to the surgeon's needle and knife when he was already hurting, but a special mark had formed on Jed's right cheek from that procedure from which I drew courage for the job at hand—a purple, heart-shaped scar.

Jed's "Purple Heart," a permanent reminder of his courage during that recent painful bedside procedure, seemed to still my heart and steady my hands. I quickly snipped off the injured toes, plucked out a few tarry feathers, ran cold water over the bleeding feet, and then poured iodine from our first-aid kit over the wounds to prevent infection. Wrapping the pigeon's feet with sterile gauze, Jed applied gentle pressure to PT's feet while I finished my inspection. Several coils of finer fishing line were looped around the bird's neck and wings.

"What a good boy," Jed assured his patient when the last loop fell to the floor. "That's better, aye?" He sounded so much like the caring nurse who had "rolled" the new graft on his Purple Heart every four hours that I actually smile through my tears as I cleaned up our makeshift surgical room. *Is true compassion, the desire to relieve suffering, a response learned from suffering?*

When PT's toes stopped bleeding, we bundled the bird in Brian's clean towel. Jed tucked him under his arm like a football player headed for the end zone.

"Time to fly!" Jed announced as I fumbled in my purse for keys ... and a tissue. *This business of healing is so agonizing. Why can't we all just bypass the painful parts? Everything I do reminds me how unhealed I am. Like the shepherd psalmist, I cry, "Oh that I had wings like a dove! For then I would fly away, and be at rest." Yet my greatest concern is not for me but for my little fledgling. Will the damage Jed has suffered prevent him from achieving the heights?*

Jed's gloved hands gently smoothed PT's pearly crown as we returned to Granville Island. By the time we found a parking space, the bird appeared to be asleep. As Jed placed him on the familiar cobblestones, PT flopped away awkwardly, just as he had done when he was tangled in the fish line.

"Look, Mom. He doesn't even know he's free!" Jed said, frowning with concern. "He'll be okay, though, won't he? I mean after he realizes he can still do what the other pigeons do? Like ... before his ... *umm* ... accident?"

"I think so, Jed," I said as I squeezed my son's shoulder, silently willing PT to walk, to fly. "I think that was a successful rescue."

As if on cue, Pigeon Toes straightened up and began moving his head back and forth like the other pigeons. He gingerly tested his range of motion. Stretching his neck forward, he began flapping his wings. A few seconds later, he flew upward and landed awkwardly on the ledge of a brick building above us. He folded his wings, like any other pigeon, then turned around and looked down at us. Jed folded his arms across his chest, looked up at me, and smiled as well as he could with his restricted facial mobility. At that moment, something happened that is forever etched upon my heart.

Pigeon Toes

A ray of sunshine broke through the clouds and highlighted Jed. It gradually widened to include his pigeon. I could not have captured the true intensity of the moment on film, not even if I'd had a camera with me on that unforgettable day. That shaft of light from the golden sunset warmed my whole being. It was as if God was assuring me that my son was growing a caring heart. Suddenly, I understood that soiled gloves, surgeries, and even scars were nearly inconsequential. I was beginning to see a bigger picture.

Time stood still as my vision expanded. I was thankful for the successful rescue, but there was something so much more, now. Perhaps my son had envisioned many things that I had been unable to see since his burn accident. No doubt, he had envisioned a successful rescue even before he attempted to catch this bird, but there was more. Having been through the fire, he had learned to disdain earthbound non-essentials, the crutches on which I was still leaning. I struggled to relax my throat as I continued to behold the heavenly phenomenon of light surrounding Jed. I wanted to give my little soldier some words of encouragement.

"He's a new bird, son," I finally managed to speak above a whisper. "I think he might be thanking you for rescuing him. He won't be exactly the same as before his accident, but his scars won't prevent him from doing whatever he needs to do."

"Oh, yeah, Mom," Jed assured me with a casual toss of his gloved hand. "Scars are nothing."

For the complete version of Jed's healing journey and touching love story, read *Rainbow in the Flames*.

Our Heroes

Here's a hand to the boy who has courage
To do what he knows to be right;
When he falls in the way of temptation,
He has a hard battle to fight.
Who strives against self and his comrades
Will find a most powerful foe
All honor to him if he conquers.
A cheer for the boy who says "No!"

There's many a battle fought daily
That the world knows nothing about;
There's many a brave little soldier
Whose strength puts a legion to rout.
And he who fights sin singlehanded
Is more of a hero, I say
Than he who leads soldiers to battle
And conquers by arms in the fray.

Be steadfast, my boy, when you're tempted
Not to do what you know to be right.
Stand firm by the colors of manhood,
And you'll overcome in the fight.
"The right," be your battle cry ever
In waging the warfare of life,
And God, who knows who are the heroes,
Will give you the strength for the strife.

—*Phoebe Cary*

The Open Cage

He healeth the broken in heart, and bindeth up their wounds.

—Psalm 147:3

I have never heard a story to equal the magnitude of Colleen's abuse. The emotional scars of her early years still claw at her, but like her bird friends, she has learned the secret of placing total trust in her Father. This is a firsthand account of how one woman discovered, and relies on, the remarkable ability of birds to heal her wounded spirit and open the cage that would have prevented her from finding happiness.

I had never seen her before. She wasn't wearing clothing that would attract attention. I didn't even notice the color of her hair. I only saw the tears she tried to hide. I worried when she disappeared, wondering if I would be able to find her again in the crowd before the day was through. Instead, she found me. First she apologized for walking out earlier, explaining how difficult it is for her to risk coming to a public place where someone or something might impact her emotionally. Then she told me an incredible story, though she knew nothing of my keen intense interest in the very subject that she was about to share.

"When a message presses too close to my heart, as your husband's did this morning," Colleen explained, "I just have to get outside."

"So you are on a healing journey?" I asked.

"Yes," she said, while nodding.

"Tell me: what is helping you heal?"

"Birds!" Her tears twinkled.

Now, those who know me best realize that I absolutely cannot resist a true-life story of healing, especially when it involves birds! Colleen seemed willing to share her heart, so we sought a quiet corner. As I listened to the account of her childhood, I became convinced that Colleen would not be alive today if she hadn't found a way to release her frustrations.

Like so many stories of abuse, Colleen's problems were forced upon her as a child, leaving her to rage at the God that she thought, until then, was her protector. The longer the abuse continued, the more trapped she felt, until like a caged wild bird her spirit was broken. Fear silenced her from reporting her abuser. Unable to concentrate on her lessons, she dropped out of public high school and struggled through special education classes until she graduated. As she entered her teen years, she found it more and more difficult to believe in a heavenly Father's love.

"I began to wonder what love really was," Colleen told me with tears in her eyes. "I felt so empty. Someone I had trusted hurt me. Although I was relocated, I was in emotional turmoil, confused, and helpless to escape my fears. Then, when I was in my early twenties, a psychiatrist helped me verbalize my feelings. When he was able to convince me that the damage I had experienced was not my fault and that other people also suffer in a similar way, a tiny ray of light pierced the entrance to my dark tunnel. I was relieved to know the truth, yet I felt I needed a friend to walk beside me, to pull me through the confusion. *Could anyone do that for me?* I wondered. What I really wanted was to know the God of Psalm 46:1, who could be 'my refuge and strength, a very present help in trouble.'

"For the first time, I realized that I was not alone in what I had suffered, and I began to wish I could understand real love. When I heard that God was love I really tried to believe it, but my pain was too intense.

"'If you are love,' I raged at God, 'then show me! You say you love me, but what *is* love? I have been told I was loved, and that same person abused me. I feel so empty inside!' Linda, it was in that instant that God spoke to me."

"Look at the birds, Colleen!" God said clearly. My heart burned with a warmth of feeling I had never known before. God, my heavenly Father, was speaking to me! "Listen to the birds. Study them carefully, from the tiniest to the biggest, then you will see how I want to love and protect you."

"Since that day, I have made a conscious effort to study birds. I joined the local bird club, bought a colorful field guide, and was soon able to identify many species. I not only learned the names of the birds, but I received numerous lessons from my bird friends that I could clearly see applied to my own situation. Bible verses, such as Psalm 91:4—'He shall cover thee with His feathers, and under his wings shalt thou trust'—became real to me when I observed the little hens protecting their chicks. The young ones were safe beneath her wings. It's difficult to describe to someone else, but I feel God's protection when I see how the birds are so careful and tender with their little families.

"When my husband, Larry, senses that my 'caged' feeling is returning, he gives me a gentle hug, an encouraging word, but he doesn't stop there. He loads up our four-wheeler and we head out to Duck Lake. I hold tightly to him as we ride the quad for the last couple of miles overland. I used to be a little afraid, but now, when I feel the wind in my face and see bright orioles and bluebirds flying from tree to tree, I sense a freedom I never dreamed I could know. Gratefully, I squeeze Larry a little tighter. He's my gift from God. He is helping to spring my cage door open.

"It's not a long trip to the lake, but it takes us longer than it might take others because we are always stopping to see new wonders along the way. Larry is so good to me. He has accepted me, damage and all. More than anyone else, he is helping me heal by gently urging my progress. We're celebrating twenty-five years together! Once, while we were camping, we held hands while we watched a brilliant meteor shower. Another night, sitting by the fire overlooking the lake, we heard the loons calling back and forth to each other. It was so comforting. Moments like these fill me with love. I can never forget these healing experiences."

"Colleen," I interrupt, "do you know that I collect stories of how birds help people to heal?"

"No."

"Would you mind writing your story for me?"

"Oh, I can't write, Linda!" Colleen protests. "I have a severe learning disability."

"I wouldn't wonder after what you have been through! Maybe we can work on it together?"

As we hug, she promises to mail me some of her notes.

A few weeks later, I received a large manila envelope in the mail. Inside are Colleen's notes, written as she sat beside her favorite lake.

> A deer stands quietly beneath the swaying spruce trees. Snowcapped mountains rise against a brilliant sky. A harlequin duck swims past, unafraid. Tree swallows are catching insects for their young. Goldfinches and white-crowned sparrows are singing in the leafy green trees. The mountain bluebirds are sitting on the fence posts singing. I see, hear, and feel the peace and quietness. The wind is blowing softly on my face. Taking a deep breath, I smell the different blossoms on the various trees. I gaze out onto the quiet waters. I see many ducks. At first, they all look alike. I search my bird book for some identifying characteristics. What color! What beauty God has surrounded me with! There is a cinnamon teal with deep reddish-brown head and a red eye. I see some ruddy ducks; black head, white cheek patch, light blue bill. There are many other water birds: ring-necked ducks, redheads, blue—and green-winged teals, and northern shovelers. The bufflehead dives under water and pops back up, its glossy purple head and white cheek patches glistening in the

sunlight. Coots paddle busily along the near shore. On the far edge of the lake, I see a pelican swimming, his characteristic orange beak catching the afternoon light. I catch my breath as the binoculars reveal a beautiful great white egret stepping gracefully out from behind his cover in a quiet eddy not far from me. I see a flock of snow geese come in for a landing.

What's that I hear? A big splash! An osprey is diving for fish! Far in the distance, the red-necked grebes and trumpeter swans are calling to each other. An eagle soars overhead. With seemingly little effort, he rises higher and higher. As I watch him, the tune written to Isaiah 40:31 is in my heart: "They that wait upon the Lord shall renew their strength; they shall mount up with wings as eagles; they shall run and not be weary; and they shall walk, and not faint. Teach me, Lord, teach me Lord, to wait."

Colleen can't always be outside. She has many health problems and often is unable to leave home. If she is feeling well enough, but Larry is working, Colleen sometimes goes out birding with another friend, a woman who has also suffered pain similar to Colleen's. Together, she and Colleen are prying open the door of her cage. The two of them speak of their mutual frustrations. They share laughter and sometimes shed a few tears about their struggle to keep the cage door open so that they can stretch their wings. Mundane chores, requiring little effort for most folks, cause those who are wounded in spirit to cautiously test the door of their cage several times a day, to see if it really is open before they can tackle the simplest of chores.

"We're crock pots in a microwave world," Colleen tells her friend. They laugh. They cry together, too. Life tends to move more slowly for a survivor. Colleen shares advice, with her bird friends as well as others who struggle with the injustices of life.

Find your quiet place. My favorite place is in the great outdoors, but you go wherever you discover peace in your soul. There will be days when you are confused. You might wonder when the pain will end and whether life is worth living. Never doubt that life is worth the effort! Don't keep your angry feelings bottled up inside or you will become a ticking time bomb! There will be tough times, but you will make it! Study the birds. I pray that you, like me, will also see God's promises fulfilled and sense His healing hand upon you. You are never alone—it only *seems* that way. There is *someone* who will be there when trouble and fear pile up and seem to jam your cage door shut. You are special! No one can replace you! You were created for a very special purpose! Don't lose hope! My Special Friend helped me! My cage door is open! He will open yours too!

"Get Well Card from Heaven"

During a recent phone conversation, Colleen told me about her "get well card from heaven." While she was healing from her second hip replacement surgery, Larry placed her gently in a recliner, arranged some food and books within reach, opened the curtains and the window, and left for work.

"It was a beautiful spring day, Linda," Colleen said. "From my armchair I could see a portion of our plum tree. Its pink blossoms were framed by a brilliant blue sky. The sun was streaming through the window, but as they often do when I am indoors, ghosts from the past began to invade my thoughts. Did I ever feel trapped! I struggled to resist the panic that threatened to overwhelm me. I closed my eyes and prayed aloud.

"'Lord, You know how much I'd love to be outside in the sunshine today and to hear the bird songs. Nevertheless, not my will, Lord.'

The Open Cage

"I attempted to resign myself to the fact that I would not be discovering any of my treasures in the trees this day, when, at about ten o'clock, a soft, trilling sound came to me through the open window. My heart skipped a beat. Could it possibly be my special favorite? I held my breath. The song came again, a little clearer. I was sure I recognized the song, but would the singer climb *just a little higher* so that I could see him? His beautiful song increased in volume until it sounded as if that little winged messenger from heaven was sitting right in my room!

"I couldn't remain seated. I struggled to my feet and inched my way across the room, supporting myself on pieces of furniture, until I reached the window. I peeked eagerly outside. There, perched among the pink blossoms of our plum tree, was the most colorful bird in all of Canada: a lazuli bunting! Singing! For *me*! I not only heard the song, I got the message!"

> Throw open the windows of the soul and let the sunlight of God's love come in to illuminate the darkened chambers of the mind. The most exalted spiritual truths may be brought home to the heart through the things of nature. The birds of the air, the flower of the field in their glowing beauty, the springing grain, the fruitful branches of the vine, the trees putting forth their tender buds, the glorious sunset, the crimson clouds predicting a fair tomorrow, the recurring seasons—all these may teach us precious lessons of trust and faith (*Counsels on Health*, E. White, 1951, Pacific Press).
>
> The great provider for man and beast opens His hand and supplies all His creatures. The birds of the air are not beneath His notice. He does not drop the food into their bills, but He makes provision for their needs. They must gather the grains He has scattered for them. They must prepare the material for their little nests. They must feed their

young. They go forth singing to their labor, for "your heavenly Father feedeth them." And "are ye not much better than they?" (*Steps to Christ*, E. White, 1956, Pacific Press).

"God told me that day, as I leaned on the windowsill and listened to the healing song of my special bunting, "I am with you today, Colleen." So many times when I have been tempted to get discouraged He has assured me over and over again, "You are *never* alone." Often that assurance comes to me by way of a bird.

"And would you believe it, Linda? That faithful little, blue bunting came again at four o'clock that same afternoon, just to make *sure* I got the message!"

Under His Wings

Under His wings I am safely abiding;
Though the night deepens and tempests are wild,
Still I can trust Him I know He will keep me
He has redeemed me and I am His child.

Under His wings
Under His wings
Who from His love can sever?
Under His wings my soul shall abide
Safely abide forever

Under His wings what a refuge in sorrow
How the heart yearningly longs for its rest!
Often when earth has no balm for my healing
There I find comfort and there I am blest.

Under His wings, O what precious enjoyment!
There will I hide till life's trials are o'er;
Sheltered protected, no evil can harm me;
Resting in Jesus I'm safe ever more.

—*W. O. Cushing*

Trill

Thou art my hiding place; thou shalt preserve me from trouble; thou shalt compass me about with songs of deliverance.

—Psalm 32:7

The friendliness of the little hermit thrush was peculiar. He was a refreshing influence, a free spirit who chose to come close. Meredith learned invaluable lessons from his visit, including heavenly truths about the joys of restoration.

June 23 had been unseasonably hot for British Columbia. Meredith* and I collapsed beside each other on the porch swing as the setting sun touched the foothills of the Rockies on our western horizon. Familiar evening songs soothed us: a yellow warbler, a robin, a hermit thrush. Their work was done for the day too.

"Thank you for your help in the greenhouse today, Meredith."

"I enjoy it so much!" Meredith smiled shyly. "For as long as I can remember, I've wanted to work in a greenhouse. It feels to me as if I was meant to find you folks. I am so thankful to be here."

Meredith was my gift from God that year. Not only did she do whatever I asked of her, she anticipated the next job as if she had grown up in the greenhouse! She expertly groomed flower baskets and trays of plants that had reached maturity and were ready to sell. She made deliveries, organized our inventory of identification tags, and kept a multitude of miscellaneous details in order. I even entrusted her with watering the greenhouse, a chore that is not as simple as it looks since the assorted plants require differing amounts of water.

"Look!" I whispered to Meredith as the sun dipped below the horizon. "Over there! On the edge of the roof!" A hermit thrush had flown from his hiding place among the aspens, and settled on the woodshed. As we watched, he released his evening song, the same cascade of heavenly music that we had often heard echoing in the surrounding forest.

"That's the most beautiful sound I've ever heard," Meredith said softly as our diminutive soloist concluded his concert. "I've missed bird songs while I was living in the city these past few years. I can't count how many times I have dreamed of a place where I could live simply: tend a garden, eat healthfully, heat with wood, and escape from the world of virtual reality. I'm so thankful to be here. I can feel myself healing. It's an answer to my prayer."

Raised by her godly grandmother, Meredith had tried for several years to find her niche in several large cities. Urged by employers and friends to compromise her convictions, her stress level had spiraled out of control. She began to wonder if life was worth the effort. Attempting to escape the controversy she sensed within herself, she returned her roots in eastern Canada. Before she came to our home, she had been searching for the place she knew, in her heart, that she needed to find. She wanted to live in a country setting where she would not only have a sense of belonging, but be of help to someone. When she had talked to her city friends about her dream of living a simple life in the country, they did not understand the longing in her heart.

"People don't live that way anymore," they told her. "You need to learn to fit into today's world. Find a good job. Make a living. Sell yourself if you need to. Get ahead." The remarks that were designed to discourage her from leaving the city actually made her more determined to escape.

When she discovered my husband Jere's book *(You Can Survive!)* in her grandmother's bookcase, and read about so many important lessons to be learned from country living, she felt that Jere's words were directed at her. When she phoned us, Jere detected the hidden plea in her soft voice.

"Come on out for a visit, Meredith," Jere urged. "We have plenty of room. Would you like to learn about running a greenhouse?"

"I've *always* wanted to work in a greenhouse."

"Well, it's the beginning of our greenhouse season right now," Jere explained. "You can learn the business while you help my wife do some transplanting."

She came. She slept. She worked. She slept. She hid her pain, but we sensed it in a stifled tear, a sigh, and in her desire to be alone a little too often. We also saw some encouraging signs of healing. Back in the city, she had tried so hard to become what she was not: a player of games, a party girl, and a ladder climber. It was so rewarding to see her become what she was meant to be: a country girl with a love for simplicity. As she filled trays with growing medium, planted seeds, and transplanted seedlings, she told me of the object lessons that spoke to her heart. What a joy it was to see her rediscover a zest for life, and for God's great book of nature.

"This is how I've always wanted to live!" she had told me as we sat on the porch swing the evening that the little hermit thrush sang to us. "Thank you so much for letting me come."

"Meredith, if I had known how much you wanted to get out of that big city, I'd have come down and rescued you myself!" I assured her.

"There must be others, don't you think?" she questioned. "How do we reach the ones who don't yet know about the joys of country living?"

"We must wait," I cautioned, "until they too are ready to sit quietly and listen to the birds." The thrush swooped down in search of grubs among the bark chips that layered the ground in front of the woodshed. "We need to name that bird. A hermit thrush is not generally as friendly as this one. We might see him again."

"His name is Trill—the sound of his song," Meredith said with conviction.

"The perfect name!" I agreed.

Trill's morning and evening sacrifice of praise was an audible treasure: a melodious cascade to hold in the inner ear, much like the splendor of rainbow captured in the mind's eye. Then tragedy struck.

Shortly before sunrise on June 25, as Jere and I were reading upstairs in bed and listening to Trill's morning melody, we heard an ominous *thump* against our bedroom window. Then silence.

I raised up on my elbow to peek out the window. There, on the roof of our front porch, lay the crumpled form of a hermit thrush.

"Jere!" I panicked. "It's Trill!"

"Oh no," Jere groaned. "How can you be sure?"

"Listen."

Painful silence.

"Let's pray," Jere said.

"Oh, Lord," I begged as I fell to my knees. "Please help us save this little bird. Trill is so special. Show us what to do. Amen."

From our bed, I watched over the still form of Trill while Jere quickly dressed and went in search of a ladder to lean against the roof. While he was gone, I removed the screen and reached out the window. I stretched as far as I could, but the injured bird was still far beyond my grasp—breathing but not moving. *Hmmm....* What if I climbed out the window?

"But Lord, I'm afraid of heights...." I objected weakly. Fear stiffened my fingers as I wrestled with the window screen. As I placed my foot on the roof, Trill regained consciousness and struggled to right himself. He flopped over twice and rolled down the roof dangerously close to the edge. Then he was still, his beak pressed against the roof, wings outstretched. One more flop and he would fall, perhaps to his death. My heart surged with longing. Barefooted and in my nightgown, I climbed out the window and onto the porch roof where I slowly inched downward until I reached the motionless bird. I scooped him up and pressed him gently to my heart.

Now what? The ground looked dizzyingly distant. The edge of the roof magnetized me making me I feel as if I would fall. I glanced behind me.

The window looked much farther away than I thought it would. Could I make it back? My legs began to shake. I took a deep breath and closed my eyes against the fearful reality of my predicament.

"Linda! What *are* you *doing*?" From the window behind me, my husband's voice sounded incredulous.

"Help me, Jere!" I whimpered without opening my eyes.

"Don't panic!" Jere soothed "I'm right behind you. Back up slowly."

I inched backward for what seemed like an hour before I felt the windowsill press against my back. I turned and slowly handed Trill through the window to Jere, then I tumbled backwards onto our bed, weak with fear and exertion.

"Blow him with your hair drier," Jere advised. "He's in shock. That'll warm him up."

I hummed snatches of "Londonderry Air" while I warmed the precious songster against my chest, with my blow drier on low. I felt him grip my little finger. He was coming to....

I walked down the hallway and tapped on Meredith's bedroom door. Her eyes grew wide with concern when she saw the bundle in my hands.

"Oh, no!" She breathed deeply. "Is it...Trill?"

"Pretty sure. He's the only hermit thrush I know who visits us."

"What can I do?"

"Hold him. Keep him warm while I get dressed."

Meredith tenderly caressed the little bird and spoke softly to him.

As I dressed, I pictured Meredith encouraging Trill with lessons from her own story: "Sometimes hurtful things happen as the result of unwise decisions. We might hit a barrier, but the Lord will never forsake us. No matter how hard life gets, it's still worth the living, Trill. Hang on. Please hang on."

I hurried back to Meredith's room where I found Trill snuggled down in caring hands. When I scratched his head, he opened one eye, then struggled to perch on Meredith's finger.

Trill

Before long he flew toward the window and landed on a dahlia that Meredith was nursing back to health. Gently, Meredith gathered him back into the safety of her hands and we went outside. I clicked a few pictures of Trill before he focused on his familiar aspen grove and flew away.

The next evening at sunset, after another long, hot day in the greenhouse, Meredith and I were again sitting together on the porch swing when Trill returned. He swooped down from the roof of the woodshed onto the lawn, snapped a bug out of the air directly in front of us, and flew back into the woods. Happy ending!

Well, it was a happy ending until he flew against our living room window a few days later. Meredith picked him up from the porch and warmed him, but he was weak and unresponsive for nearly an hour. We sat on the porch steps, hoping that the sounds of his forest friends would coax him awake. Slowly, he gathered his senses, but clung to Meredith's finger much longer than before. At last, he chose to fly, but when he headed back toward his woodland home, he was barely above ground level and the woods remained silent for eight days.

Then, there he was again, back on the woodshed serenading us with his evening song! He hopped to the ground in front of us, snatched a bug, and disappeared into the forest.

Before Meredith and I stopped swinging that evening I had considered some deep thoughts: the joy of restoration, of how God uses the hardships of life to renovate a heart, and about my dream of creating a sanctuary for those who, like Trill and Meredith, just needed a quiet place to heal. Could I do anything more than just *be there*?

Yes, there was one thing I could do. I could pray. It does make a difference. It had helped Trill. And Meredith.

---

*pseudonym

Into the Light

The eagle of the Alps is sometimes beaten down
by the tempest into the narrow defiles of the mountains.
Storm clouds shut in this mighty bird of the forest,
their dark masses separating her from the sunny heights
where she has made her home.

Her efforts to escape seem fruitless.
She dashes to and fro, beating the air with her strong wings,
and waking the mountain echoes with her cries.

At length, with a note of triumph, she darts upward,
and, piercing the clouds, is once more in the clear sunlight,
with the darkness and tempest far beneath.

So we may be surrounded with difficulties,
discouragement, and darkness.
Falsehood, calamity, injustice, shut us in.
There are clouds that we cannot dispel.
We battle with circumstances in vain.
There is one, and but one, way of escape.
The mists and fogs cling to the earth;
beyond the clouds God's light is shining.
Into the sunlight of His presence
we may rise on the wings of faith.

—E. White

The Sparrow's Song

*Are not five sparrows sold for two farthings,
and not one of them is forgotten before God?
But even the very hairs of your head are numbered.
Fear not therefore: ye are of more value than many sparrows.*

—Luke 12:6, 7

The trouble could not be resolved. Mckenna* had prayed and prayed, but it seemed that her problem was too big, even for God. That He had not answered her many prayers for relief only added more weight to her burden of discouragement. Someone who was not so badly in need of an encouraging song might have missed it that day, but for the sorrowing woman the sparrow's message came through loud and clear. Every single word.

To a country woman, color is energy. Her strength arrives in a variety of tones: in springtime, the brilliant green of her favorite weeping willow sparks hope for the resurrection of freshly buried seed. In the summer, her healthy blush reflects the blossoming geraniums that she protected through the cold winter months. Gratefulness puts the golden twinkle in her eye when the harvest is complete in the fall. Life, it seems, is a series of preparations, and it had always been during the white months that

Mckenna hungered most for color. Oblivious to subzero temperatures, she gazed in wonder at the northern lights by night, and purposely disturbed the glittering snow diamonds on her walks during the short winter days. She, like other wives in her community, hungrily devoured each new tint that arose from the challenging dynamics of farm life.

This year was different. Somewhere between winter and spring, a dark shadow had vacuumed up all the colors. A great sorrow had left Mckenna feeling wilted. Her sunny outlook had faded. Before the hay crop was knee-high, her cheeks had paled. Life was a drudgery.

Obviously, the problem was too big to solve, even for God, who had not answered her prayers. She kept going through the motions of living—she had to—but her soul had shriveled. Mckenna hadn't meant to turn her back on God. She still went to church and smiled, even as her heart was breaking. The sermons were nice, but she could not allow herself to be touched too deeply by them. The ache was so much worse when she allowed herself to feel. Secretly, however, she longed for a sign that would assure her that her Father cared.

It was time to collect the hay bales. A country woman does what is expected, but Mckenna's heart felt like one of the bales that dotted the field: crimped, bound, bleached, and lifeless. As usual, she would drive the big eighteen-wheeler through the fields while her son, in the tractor, loaded the round bales onto the trailer. It was a good crop. There had been plenty of rain. She should be more appreciative. She knew that in her head, but this unrelenting cloud of depression had sucked her energy. She used to appreciate breakfast, but today it had tasted like … hay.

Mckenna climbed into the big Kenworth and closed the door. There was a certain comfort in the familiarity of the old truck—tangible reminders of happier times. Tears stung the corners of her eyes. She blinked resolutely, gripped the steering wheel, pressed on the clutch, and turned the key. As the motor warmed, Mckenna rested her head against the familiar vibration of the steering wheel. An unbidden picture came to her mind.

The Sparrow's Song

She pictured herself leaning against Him, feeling the surge of His heart. His invitation to trust Him with her pain filled the cab of the eighteen-wheeler. The time was right. Mckenna could not bear His closeness without responding. She was already bowed, and it did not seem so difficult to surrender.

"Lord, help me?" she whispered, not knowing how else to say what she needed. She wasn't really expecting an answer, but she waited in silence, just in case.

She heard nothing but the lugging of the diesel engine. When it sounded warm, Mckenna lifted her head. That's when she saw him. A little, brown sparrow had landed on the driver's side of the bug guard. He'd been waiting patiently for her to look up. In spite of the noisy vibrations, he delivered his message.

Mckenna had known the words to his song her whole life. Her pain had smothered it for a while, but suddenly the words came flooding back to her.

His Eye Is on the Sparrow

Why should I feel discouraged, why should the shadows come,
Why should my heart be lonely, and long for heaven and home,
When Jesus is my portion? My constant friend is He:
His eye is on the sparrow, and I know He watches me;
His eye is on the sparrow, and I know He watches me.

Refrain:
I sing because I'm happy,
I sing because I'm free,
For His eye is on the sparrow,
And I know He watches me.

Just a Little Higher

"Let not your heart be troubled," His tender word I hear,
And resting on His goodness, I lose my doubts and fears;
Though by the path He leadeth, but one step I may see;
His eye is on the sparrow, and I know He watches me;
His eye is on the sparrow, and I know He watches me.

Whenever I am tempted, whenever clouds arise,
When songs give place to sighing, when hope within me dies,
I draw the closer to Him, from care He sets me free;
His eye is on the sparrow, and I know He watches me;
His eye is on the sparrow, and I know He watches me.

—Civilla D. Martin

In that little, brown flash of time, Mckenna glimpsed eternity. Her eyes, her cheeks, and her heart, were cleansed. She smiled. She had to! The sparrow seemed to be waiting for it. He knew just how long to stay—just long enough for her to see the dark spot on his chest confirming that he was, indeed, a song sparrow. He would leave in the same manner he had come: in the fullness of time. Like apples of gold in pictures of silver, he left his song for Mckenna. Was this her sign? Mckenna has something to say about that.

"Sometimes, God's messages are rather direct. Other times, they are imbedded in nature. In either case, when I take time to listen, He shouts His love. The sparrow that landed on the Kenworth that day could have just come to rest its weary (but curious) self on a most unusual (and very noisy) tree. It could be argued that God had nothing to do with it. It was just a natural happening. How interesting, then, that it has never happened again and that it came precisely at the time I was attempting to 'pray through' what I look back on as the lowest valley of my life!

"The scientist in me can't help wondering how God motivates His creatures to do His bidding. There are amazing stories of animals saving human lives, but what goes on in a bird's head? Did God appear in some

The Sparrow's Song

form to a flock of sparrows in the nearby tree at the edge of our hayfield and ask for volunteers? Could one little, brave-hearted bird have gulped down his fear, raised his tiny wing in pure, unadulterated love for His Master, and said, 'I'll go, Sir! Anything for You, Sir!' Or does God use a more direct approach? Did He fiercely whisper His command to a single bird as it frolicked on the currents of the wind in the hayfield that day? 'You there! Go land on that big Kenworth! Sing your heart out!'

"All I really know is that I received the message that God loved me, that I mattered to Him, that I was not alone, that He truly cared. It was exactly what this countrywoman needed. I can never think about that day without feeling heaven's warmth ... as if I am being enfolded by the Comforter. Yes, I believe."

---

*pseudonym

A Perfect World

I'd wish for you a perfect world
Where words would not offend,
Where friends were true, and skies so blue
Held bird songs without end.
But you hurt me, and I hurt you;
From straining heartstrings hurled,
The hurtful word that we have heard—
It's not a perfect world.

Alas! Is there no perfect place
Where one is not alone,
Where words of war and hate are naught,
Nor songs of minor tone?
Yes! There's a world where tears are dried
By God's own gentle touch.
That perfect world can be our own!
We need it, oh, so much!

Oh, perfect world where hearts are healed
Where Leaves of Life are mine!
Where, thoughts and acts in
His control, Words echo the divine.
This perfect world is offered free—
No distant debt to pay.
With self-surrendered, we might live
In that perfect world today!

—L. Franklin

Out of My Shell

"He brought me up also out of an horrible pit, out of the miry clay, and set my feet upon a rock, and established my goings. And he hath put a new song in my mouth ..."

—Psalm 40:2, 3

Arley's depression had been deepening for years. Her children had tried everything they knew to lift their mother out of the mysterious blackness that was slowly smothering the life out of her. What could a comical blue bird do for her that they could not?

Like a feather from a broken wing, my spirit spiraled downward. *Just discouragement,* I thought. *It will pass.* My kids thought so too. That is, until I was finally diagnosed with a full-blown case of clinical depression.

I lived in a deep chasm of unrelenting fear and turmoil. Only those who have been there know what it's like. For several years, every accusation I had ever heard from every man I had ever known was piled onto me. They stuck like Velcro. Many nights I dreamed that I was living in a dark well. I could see that the lid was closing, but I had no power to climb out or to prevent the spot of light from gradually shrinking away to nothingness far above me. Nothing helped—not encouraging words, not invitations to dinner with the kids, not books, not my psychiatrist's prescription pills, and not one word of his well-thought-out advice. Eventually, I came to dread leaving home even for necessary grocery items.

While it was true that I did not have a pleasant home life as a kid and had, consequently, looked for love in all the wrong places, I knew that others with similar backgrounds seemed to be living normal lives. Maybe it was because my nest was empty. All six of my chicks had flown the coop. It's not as if I was abandoned though. The kids were attentive, but they just didn't really need me anymore.

Certain diseases can cause depression, but no abnormalities were revealed on any of my blood tests. Whatever it was that was causing my hopelessness, one thing was sure: I was not myself. I had always been energetic. Eventually, it didn't matter to me if I stayed in bed all day or not. So I did. After about five years of gloom, it seemed I might as well accept life as it was: very dark.

I had even quit praying about getting better. Attending church was out of the question. A friend once convinced me to accept an invitation to sing. I came to church, but I started shaking uncontrollably in the foyer and ran all the way back home! No matter how often, or how convincingly, my Christian friends implored, I just couldn't face the public. I never returned to church. Except for the painful iron band of unrelenting pressure that had permanently affixed itself around my head, I was coping well enough. Since there was no hope for recovery, and things were as they would always be, I accepted my plight. I might well be still living that lie today but for one loving and lovable little bird.

My granddaughter, Alicia, had asked her mother, my daughter Melody, for a budgie. Melody didn't realize what a negative impact the little bird would make on her world. For starters, her beloved scented candles had to be stored in the cupboard for fear of the perfumed smoke harming the bird. Then, in spite of her daughter's promise to care for the budgie, Melody found herself cleaning the cage and feeding, and watering the bird when Alicia became disenchanted. At our annual Thanksgiving dinner, from which I had absented myself, Melody mentioned the big mistake to her youngest sister, Janie.

"Hey, Mel," said Janie after listening patiently to Melody's tale of woe, "why don't you give the budgie to Mom? Goodness knows she could use some color in her life, and she has always loved animals!"

Melody was only too happy for her sister to pick up the bird and bring him to me.

I was my usual self, not in a particularly cheerful mood, when Janie knocked on my door. But one look at the beautiful, teal-blue budgie melted my heart. Did he need me? I hope I said thank-you as I closed the door. My children, bless their hearts, had tried repeatedly to reach into my darkness, but my fall was so complete that I was unable to respond to human word or touch.

Dickie Bird was pretty small, as far as angels go, but he was strong in the ways I needed. Like the softest down, he snuggled into the cold places of my heart and warmed me from the inside out. I didn't know it then, but he would accomplish what no one had been able to do for me in more than five long years. He didn't try to prop me up; he just loved me. He neither flattered nor condemned. Looking back, I needed him much more than he needed me, and I didn't even realize what he was doing until his job was nearly done.

I hadn't been on a schedule for years, but the very morning after I hung Dickie's cage in the living room I found myself getting out of bed—before noon! Over the next days, I awoke earlier and earlier so as not to miss the early morning sun spill over those beautiful, teal feathers. It was a color that invited my touch. One morning, as I changed the paper in his cage, I tentatively stroked his back. He turned his head toward me but did not shrink away. He listened carefully while I began talking. Before our first session was over, I was telling him some pretty dark secrets, things no one else, not even my therapist, knew. Dickie didn't judge me. He offered joy. He touched my broken places, and my broken places began to heal.

Within the first couple of months, Dickie had learned a "wolf whistle." Then he began repeating his name: "Dickie Bird, Dickie Bird." One day he stopped me in my tracks with, "Hi, buddy!" I surprised myself by laughing aloud for the first time in months—maybe years.

I was afraid to admit it to myself for fear the spell would break, but I knew my outlook was changing. My little, blue angel helped me decide to return to where the smiles and hugs of my church family awaited me, and I was able to accept casual friendships without interpreting a brother's squeeze as anything more than the apostle Paul's "holy kiss."

Some symptoms of my depression were slower to disappear than others; in particular, the inability to concentrate on more than one thing at a time and always muttering under my breath. I was in the midst of an intense conversation with myself when I walked outside forgetting that Dickie Bird, was on my shoulder. Away flew my angel! Fortunately, he only flew a short distance and returned to my shoulder! I quickly went back in the house and placed him safely in his cage. This incident snapped me to attention, and from that day, I became cognizant of my surroundings. I awakened from my hazy, dreamlike state.

Dickie Bird was a pesky little fellow, with equal portions of curiosity and devilment. If I happened to leave him out of his cage, which I often did when I went to get the mail, he would holler a loud, *"Hell-o!"* from his second favorite spot, on top of the refrigerator, when I returned. One of his favorite tricks was to wait until I was absorbed in washing dishes, quietly find his way to the top of the refrigerator without me noticing, then squawk loudly right beside me. It never failed to scare the daylights out of me!

He thoroughly enjoyed showering under the kitchen tap. One day while I was washing dishes, he decided to bathe. He attempted to land on my hand, which was slick with dish soap. He landed, *plunk*, in my dishwater! I grabbed him, rinsed him off, and wrapped him in a towel. We sat down together for a while. After all, dishes are not as important as a friendly chat when you've had a good scare. I knew he would be okay when he climbed up on my shoulder and started smearing my glasses with his tongue, one of his favorite pastimes.

My creativity returned. I soon felt good enough to tackle a knitting project, something I had abandoned in the early stages of my lengthy illness. Dickie perched on my finger and tried to catch the yarn as it jerked past. I began sharing colorful potholders with my neighbors. Then I resurrected my baking skills and gave loaves of bread away. As my gift of hospitality returned, I was able to plan, prepare, and serve a good meal, which I thought I would never do again!

Most of the time, it was just Dickie and me around the kitchen table though. He enjoyed partaking of fresh fruit, if it was on my plate, but was not interested if I put it in his cage. He enjoyed several foods: romaine, scrambled eggs, toast (with butter), popcorn, hash browns, and macaroni. At first, I shredded carrots for him, but when I watched him shred his own, I realized, with a laugh, that his method was much more efficient!

Who would have thought that a budgie could pull a woman up and out of such a horrible pit of despair? But, you know, I don't begrudge my fall. Not at all. The darkness helped me appreciate the light. I am a better person for the journey. Now it's easier for me to talk to those who are discouraged. I seem to be able to listen more effectively, detecting those silent sounds that my son, JR, wrote about.

Silent Sounds

Have you heard the sound of a tear?
Have you listened to its cry?
Can you discern its lonely tone
The whispered, mournful sigh?
Have you harkened to a smile,
Enjoyed the warmth it brings?
Have you tried to understand
The quiet song it sings?

Just a Little Higher

Tears of joy are often shed
When smiles can't play the part.
And smiles are often hiding
Some great sadness of the heart.
Smiles and tears can be reversed;
Heed the broken strain—
Tears are smiles and smiles are tears;
Discernment comes with pain.

Listen, friend, and comprehend
Silent sounds—the muted sigh
In the hearts of those about you—
Joyful tears? Or smiles that cry?

—Jon Kiefiuk

    Dickie broke my shell. I now weep mostly joyful tears. You'll have to excuse me now. I have an appointment with a friend. I have several good friends, the kind who listen and don't judge. Like Dickie Bird. None of us have wings yet, but we discuss the possibilities that are open to us.

    There are days when I look up into a blue sky and can't help but think of a certain tiny angel who, one dark day, grabbed a sunbeam from heaven and wedged it, like an arrow straight and true, into a cold and lonely heart. I can still feel the warmth.

    Thank you, sweet little blue angel, for gently cracking my shell and pulling me up and out of my prison! I see that shell now for what it really was: not a protection from pain but a killer of joy.

A Rooster Named Benedict

Penny Porter

Cast me not off in the time of old age;
Forsake me not when my strength faileth.

—Psalm 71:9

"Cereal again?" Bill scowled at the heaping bowlful placed in front of him. "It looks just like what I fed those yearling bulls an hour ago ..."

"I'm sorry, honey," I said, "but we ran out of eggs again! If we had our own chickens, this wouldn't happen all the time."

"But we're ranchers," he muttered. "Ranchers raise cattle. *Farmers* raise chickens."

When you live on an Arizona ranch many miles from the nearest store, no eggs is a disaster. Our whole family loved eggs, especially Bill. He had them every morning—poached, fried, or scrambled. But, most of all, he loved eggs Benedict.

And I loved chickens, which is why I wanted some of our own. Ever since we'd bought the ranch, my mind had been filled with storybook images of a little, red hen, four golden chicks, and a magnificent rooster perched on a weathervane, welcoming the sunrise. "If we had our own chickens," I again reminded Bill, "we'd never ever run out of eggs!"

He'd heard all this before. Now he heaved a sigh of resignation. I hugged him, knowing I'd won.

While Bill proceeded to erect a chicken coop and order a weathervane, I pored through poultry catalogues with the children. A neighbor suggested buying one hundred chicks. "With your big family, you'll need that many for sure," he said, "and you can sell all the extras."

Hatcheries, I learned, mail one extra chick for every twenty-five ordered—consolation for the few that get squashed in shipping. What a relief it was that all 104 of ours survived. For variety, I'd ordered leghorns, Plymouth Rocks, Rhode Island Reds, and—my favorite of all—Araucanas. Once grown, Araucanas lay blue, buff, olive-green, and turquoise eggs. "Every day will be Easter!" I told the children.

We housed them under a heat lamp on our kitchen floor. Right away, we noticed one Araucana was bigger and bossier than the rest. Terror and confusion reigned as she chased the others from food and water. The poultry book warned, "There is always a dominant hen in a flock who fights to maintain her position as 'number one in the pecking order.'" This big chick, I decided, was "number one."

Wondering if extra handling might calm her, I cupped the chick in my hands, carried her around, and talked softly to her. To my surprise, this worked. The frantic cheeping stopped, the eyelids closed, and the tiny heart knocking at my palms finally slowed down. I also fed the chick by herself, hoping she'd eat her fill and one day lay the biggest eggs of all. In anticipation of her first egg, Bill named her Benedictine.

Six months after the chicks were delivered, our assumption that all were females proved to be flawed: we had fifty-two roosters and fifty-two hens. That many roosters heralding the dawn was a whole lot more than we could take. So we pruned the flock to one rooster: the big one, Benedictine. I renamed him Benedict.

A Rooster Named Benedict

Gradually, Benedict grew to the size of a small turkey. He was young, proud, and magnificent. As he matured, his comb and wattles deepened to a rich scarlet. He sported a glorious, multicolored cape and streaming tail feathers that flashed red, green, yellow, and glistening onyx in the Arizona sunshine. His claws were nearly as large as my hands, and his golden spurs, tipped with razor-sharp talons, glinted on the backs of his legs.

Benedict became my pet. He sought attention by untying my sneaker laces and gargling his pleasure when I produced a cookie or peanut-butter treat. He won "Best of Show" at the county fair, and in my arms he rested quietly, showing an unusual tameness for a rooster. He loved and trusted me. I loved and trusted him.

Long before the end of their first year, our Araucana hens were laying colored eggs, which sold for three dollars a dozen. Meanwhile, virile Benedict was making certain every egg was fertilized, and local farmers and 4-H enthusiasts sought those eggs for hatching to replenish their own flocks. With Benedict's help, my chickens were paying their way.

At age three, however, his status as the only rooster began going to his head. Previously, Benedict had loved the company of the hens. Now, acting like king of the roost, he started attacking any hen who dared to share his throne, which was the uppermost perch. If a hen tried to snatch a kernel of cracked corn from the feeder before he was finished, Benedict would pin her to the ground, hold fast with his terrible talons, and stab her repeatedly with his dagger-like beak.

"You shoulda kept more than one rooster," said my neighbor. "Too much breeding's addled his brain."

Soon Benedict started turning on me as well. Gone was the old trust, the contented clucking, cookie searching, and plucking at my sneaker laces. Now, following me from nest to nest, he scolded, thumped his feet, and made ghoulish, hissing sounds. Knowing his long, sharp beak could skewer my leg, I was forced to enter the coop armed with a broom, rake, or pitchfork. Even then, when his comb and wattles turned from scarlet to purple, weapons were useless. I ran.

Then one night I awakened to a chaotic squawking and screeching from the coop. Grabbing a flashlight and our shotgun, I dashed up the trail toward my flock. There, in the beam of my light, glowed the evil eyes of a ring-tailed raccoon that had tunneled into the coop. Half a dozen hens were already dead, and others lay mortally wounded. Now the raccoon clutched Benedict in his horrible claws and was preparing to rip off his head.

Though I feared Benedict, I still loved him. Gripping the flashlight between my knees, I closed my eyes and fired into the air. When I looked again, the raccoon was barreling off into the mesquite. Benedict lay still, gasping for air, his eyes wild with terror. I knelt beside him, stroked the satin feathers, and talked softly to him. Gradually he calmed down.

From that night on, I had my old Benedict back again. When we walked together from nest to nest, he gurgled approval as I filled my basket with eggs. He even puffed himself up grandly when I presented him with ten new hens to replace those he'd lost to the raccoon.

As the years passed, Benedict went faithfully about his duties. Then something turned his world—and mine—upside down. One of his hens became "broody," tired of laying. She wanted to hatch eggs instead and insisted on taking over the "favorite nest," a single box preferred by as many as a dozen different hens. Unable to gain access to this coveted spot, the other hens dropped their eggs on the concrete floor.

For some reason, "Broody" inspired in Benedict a passion beyond reason. By the hour, he would pace under her nest. He refused to eat. He lost his voice. *He's getting old, senile, and mixed up,* I thought. Then he decided to chase the more docile hens out of the other nests. Production plunged.

To make matters worse, Benedict, now ten years old, was slowing down. The hens, detecting this, started pecking at him and pulling out his wing, tail, and back feathers. Benedict sank lower and lower with each attack.

A Rooster Named Benedict

For his own protection, I decided to put him in a cage until his sores healed. I also bought two young roosters to keep the flock occupied. Broody hatched four eggs and I moved her and her chicks to the yard by our house.

When I returned Benedict to the flock, he searched for Broody for days, peering into her previous nest again and again. At the same time, he was trying to fight off the younger roosters and dominant hens. Eventually, Benedict retired to a distant corner of the chicken yard. I was too busy to pay attention to his constant molting and loss of appetite. I didn't even notice he had stopped greeting the dawn.

It was better to forget, I decided, and not say anything at all. I was relieved when Benedict's searching stopped and he retired to a distant corner of the chicken yard by day and the bottom rung of the roost at night.

Meanwhile, I enjoyed watching Broody and her four tiny chicks, particularly the one that was different from the others. "Mama, she's almost purple!" said Jaymee. "I'm going to name her Violet."

From the start, Violet was unusual. She never grew a comb or wattles, the measures of a hen's fertility. She couldn't cluck but instead peeped and chattered. Like a child, she jumped into doll buggies and waited for a ride. She sat on the swing until someone pushed. She pecked at boots and shoes until one of us picked her up.

At two, when Violet still hadn't laid an egg, the idea came to me that perhaps a rooster around might help. Using one of the younger ones was out of the question—I was afraid of them and couldn't catch them anyway. *Benedict!* I thought.

I hurried to the coop to get him. When I saw him in the darkness of the chicken house, I was saddened beyond words. With his beak open and eyes closed, his head and neck hung down like a long-forgotten rope.

Scarcely a feather remained on his twelve-year-old body, and his graying flesh was mapped in purple and green bruises, mute evidence of the constant abuse he had endured from nagging hens. *How could you let this happen!* I scolded myself. *Because he was old and ugly? Ugly? Because you were too busy to care?* "Benedict," I murmured, "please don't be dead."

At the sound of my voice, he stirred, teetering dangerously on a bottom roost. I wrapped my arms around him and lifted him carefully. When he rested his head against my shoulder, I couldn't help remembering how *beautiful* he was—when he was young.

When I reached my yard, I put him down. He lay there quietly, savoring the touch of soft grass beneath his wrinkled skin and blinking from the glare of the bright Arizona sun. After a bit, he struggled to stand. My heart ached for him.

Then Benedict spotted Violet. She was a beautiful hen, plump and round in all the right places. His head sprang up and down, and the tired eyes brightened.

I could see his heart pounding beneath the sunken ribs, fighting to loosen the chains of age. Alive with desire, he thumped his feet, clacked his beak, lifted his head, and for the first time in years, he crowed! Then my ugly, old rooster lurched through the tumbleweeds in pursuit of his new love. By nightfall, with Violet nestled at his side, Benedict was perching contentedly on the lowest branch of a tree in our yard.

For two glorious weeks, Benedict enjoyed an idyllic life with Violet. They took dust baths together, scratched for worms, and squabbled over bugs. I'd never seen him eat so well, and I put vitamins in his food in the hope of building him up a little. Before long, his arrogant strut of long ago returned, and a shimmering veil of opalescent down began to conceal the battered flesh. He also started welcoming dawn with raspy song.

Two weeks, however, was all Benedict had left. When I went out one morning to feed them, I found him motionless on the ground beneath that branch he'd shared with Violet. I tried to comfort myself by thinking, *He died happy.*

Mourning her loss, Violet spent her days searching and peeping her sorrow. She grew thin and began losing her feathers. Twelve days later, she laid her first and only egg—and then died. I reasoned there had been internal complications, but Jaymee was sure Violet had died of a broken heart.

"Violet and Benedict's baby!" Jaymee cried, picking up the large, turquoise egg lying on the front doormat. "It's in here, Mama."

We placed the egg in our commercial brooder. Twenty-one days later, Omelette hatched.

He was an adorable chick. The image of his father, he grew into the proudest of roosters. He developed a scarlet comb and wattles, rainbow-tinted tail feathers, copper-colored eyes, and golden spurs on his heels. He carried on the Benedict dynasty for years.

When the day came that Omelette too grew old, ugly, and confused, I remembered Benedict. And I took the time to stroke Omelette's ancient, torn feathers and to talk to him. Just to let the old rooster know that he too was special.

Farther Along

Farther along we'll know all about it,
Farther along we'll understand why.
Cheer up my brother, live in the sunshine,
We'll understand it all by and by.

—*W. B. Stevens/W. A. Fletcher*

We invite you to view the complete
selection of titles we publish at:
www.TEACHServices.com

We encourage you to write us
with your thoughts about this,
or any other book we publish at:
info@TEACHServices.com

TEACH Services' titles may be purchased in
bulk quantities for educational, fund-raising,
business, or promotional use.
bulksales@TEACHServices.com

Finally, if you are interested in seeing
your own book in print, please contact us at:
publishing@TEACHServices.com

We are happy to review your manuscript at no charge.

www.ingramcontent.com/pod-product-compliance
Lightning Source LLC
Chambersburg PA
CBHW020359170426
43200CB00005B/227